THIRD EDITION

NATIONAL STANDARDS FOR SPORT COACHES

QUALITY COACHES, QUALITY SPORTS

Lori Gano-Overway, PhD, CMPC
Program Director and Advisor, Coaching Education Minor
College of Health and Behavioral Studies
Department of Kinesiology
James Madison University
Harrisonburg, Virginia

Melissa Thompson, PhD, CMPC, CSCS
Professor
School of Kinesiology and Nutrition
College of Education and Human Sciences
University of Southern Mississippi
Hattiesburg, Mississippi

Pete Van Mullem, PhD
Associate Professor
Movement and Sport Sciences Division
School of Liberal Arts and Sciences
Lewis-Clark State College
Lewiston, Idaho

SHAPE
America
SOCIETY
OF HEALTH
AND PHYSICAL
EDUCATORS®

health. moves. minds.

JONES & BARTLETT
LEARNING

World Headquarters
Jones & Bartlett Learning
5 Wall Street
Burlington, MA 01803
978-443-5000
info@jblearning.com
www.jblearning.com

Jones & Bartlett Learning books and products are available through most bookstores and online booksellers. To contact Jones & Bartlett Learning directly, call 800-832-0034, fax 978-443-8000, or visit our website, www.jblearning.com.

Production Credits
VP, Product Management: Amanda Martin
Director of Product Management: Cathy Esperti
Product Assistant: Andrew Labelle
Product Coordinator: Elena Sorrentino
Project Manager: Lori Mortimer
Project Specialist: David Wile
Senior Digital Project Specialist: Angela Dooley
Director of Marketing: Andrea DeFronzo
VP, Manufacturing and Inventory Control: Therese Connell
Composition: Exela Technologies

Project Management: Exela Technologies
Cover Design: Briana Yates
Text Design: Briana Yates
Senior Media Development Editor: Troy Liston
Rights Specialist: Benjamin Roy
Cover Image (Title Page): Background: © Thanakorn_Nack/
    Shutterstock. Sports: © Lisa Kolbasa/Shutterstock.
Printing and Binding: McNaughton & Gunn

Library of Congress Cataloging-in-Publication Data
Names: Gano-Overway, Lori A., author. | Thompson, Melissa, 1979- author. | Mullem, Pete Van, author.
Title: National standards for sport coaches : quality coaches, quality sports / Lori Gano-Overway,
    Melissa Thompson, Pete Van Mullem.
Other titles: Quality coaches, quality sports
Description: Third edition. | Burlington, MA : Jones & Bartlett Learning,
    [2021] | Includes bibliographical references and index.
Identifiers: LCCN 2020023939 | ISBN 9781284205572 (paperback)
Subjects: LCSH: Coaching (Athletics)–Standards–United States. | Coaches (Athletics)–Certification–United States.
Classification: LCC GV711 .N37 2021 | DDC 796.07/7–dc23
LC record available at https://lccn.loc.gov/2020023939

6048

Printed in the United States of America
24 23 22 21 20   10 9 8 7 6 5 4 3 2 1

About SHAPE America

SHAPE America – Society of Health and Physical Educators serves as the voice for 200,000+ health and physical education professionals across the United States. The organization's extensive community includes a diverse membership of health and physical educators, as well as advocates, supporters, and 50+ state affiliate organizations.

Since its founding in 1885, the organization has defined excellence in physical education. For decades, SHAPE America's National Standards for K-12 Physical Education have served as the foundation for well-designed physical education programs across the country. The organization was also a proud member of the coalition that developed the National Health Education Standards.

SHAPE America provides programs, resources and advocacy to support health and physical educators at every grade level as they prepare all students to lead a healthy, physically active life. The organization's newest program — health. moves. minds.® — helps teachers and schools incorporate social and emotional learning so students can thrive physically *and* emotionally.

Our Vision

A nation where all children are prepared to lead healthy, physically active lives.

Our Mission

To advance professional practice and promote research related to health and physical education, physical activity, dance and sport.

To learn more, visit
www.shapeamerica.org

SHAPE America
SOCIETY OF HEALTH AND PHYSICAL EDUCATORS®

© Lisa Kolbasa/Shutterstock

Brief Contents

© Lisa Kolbasa/Shutterstock

Contents

Acknowledgments

2017-2019 Task Force (Third Edition)
Lori Gano-Overway, Task Force Chair, James Madison University
Bob Benham, CoachDevelopment.Services
Christine Bolger, United States Olympic & Paralympic Committee
Andrew Driska, Michigan State University & Institute for the Study of Youth Sport
Melissa Long, Abilene Christian University
Anthony Moreno, Eastern Michigan University
Dan Schuster, National Federation of State High School Associations
Melissa Thompson, The University of Southern Mississippi
Pete Van Mullem, Lewis-Clark State College

2015-2017 Task Force

Wade Gilbert (chair)

Kim Bodey	Mark Kovacs
Jean Côté	Mike Sheridan
Lori Gano-Overway	Melissa Thompson

2006 Task Force (Second Edition)

Jody Brylinsky (chair)

Rick Albrecht	Tim Flannery
Dennis Docheff	Cathy Sellers

1995 Task Force (First Edition)

Vern Seefeldt (chair)

Jack Acree	Pat Sullivan
Jody Brylinsky	Brent Steuerwald
David Feigley	

SHAPE America would like to recognize various quality coach education programs already implemented across the country that contributed to ideas included in this document and have helped to shape the way for quality coach education. These organizations include the Institute for the Study of Youth Sport, the Human Kinetics Coach Education Program, United States Center for Coaching Excellence and various college and national governing body coach education programs. Additionally, recognition is warranted to the many coach education programs that have demonstrated a commitment to providing quality coach education programs by seeking to accredit their program (see Appendix A). SHAPE America also acknowledges the following organizations for indicating their support for the National Standards for Sport Coaches:

SHAPE America State Affiliations

Society of Health and Physical Educators of Vermont
Society of Health and Physical Educators of Nebraska
Society of Health and Physical Educators of Pennsylvania
Society of Health and Physical Educators of New Mexico
Society of Health and Physical Educators of Idaho

Colleges and Universities

Baldwin Wallace University
Ball State University
Bridgewater College
Carson-Newman University
Central Washington University
Clarion University
Emporia State University
Fresno State University
Georgia Southern University
James Madison University
Kutztown University
Lewis-Clark State College

Michigan State University
North Dakota State University
Shawnee State University
Southern Arkansas University
Southern Methodist University
Springfield College
University of Central Florida
University of Denver
University of Idaho
University of Mary
University of Northern Colorado
University of Southern Mississippi

Other Sport Organizations

Classical Academy of Arms
Changing the Game Project
FSU COACH: Interdisciplinary Center
  for Athletic Coaching
Human Kinetics Coach Education
Iowa Basketball Coaches Association
National Interscholastic Athletic
  Administrators Association

Physical & Health Education America
Proactive Coaching LLC
Snow Valley Basketball School
Special Olympics North America
TrueSport (initiative of US Anti-Doping Agency)
US Figure Skating/Professional Skaters Association
United States Sports Academy
Virginia High School League

Through the good work of all of these organizations, SHAPE America believes that coach education will continue to evolve and gain the appropriate recognition and support it deserves.

Preface

Building upon the previous two editions of the *National Standards for Sport Coaches*, the third edition of this text outlines the standards for quality sport coaching based on the latest research and practical work in coaching science and the varied fields within kinesiology. The intent of the standards is to provide the core responsibilities coaches should possess along with supporting competencies (i.e., standards) that provide insight into the knowledge, skills, and behaviors needed to support a quality amateur sport experience for athletes. Informing coaches, sport administrators, coach educators, and coach developers about core coaching responsibilities and competencies can improve the preparation, training, and evaluation of sport coaching. Further, informing the public about the core responsibilities of sport coaches can drive expectations for quality coaching. In the end, the *National Standards for Sport Coaches* should assist in improving the sport experience for each athlete and elevate the profession of coaching.

Given the purpose of the *National Standards for Sport Coaches*, there are multiple target audiences. Coaches can use the book to identify their key responsibilities and seek opportunities for professional development based on the resources offered. Sport administrators can use the book to clarify expectations for coaches, develop formative and summative assessments for coaches, and/or identify resources to utilize in training coaches. Coach educators can use this book to frame curricula for training coaches and use the resources to inform coach education. Coach developers can use the book to support their role as a facilitator, assessor, mentor, and leader in providing up-to-date and appropriate coach development activities. Finally, athletes and their families, along with the general public, can be better informed about what core responsibilities to expect from sport coaches.

The book is organized to meet the needs of varying audiences. First, readers will review the core responsibilities for sport coaches and their corresponding standards with brief descriptions regarding the intent of each standard. Second, resources and the latest research for each standard are provided, highlighting the importance of professional development among coaches as well as program development among coach educators and coach developers. Next, how the standards might be incorporated by different sport organizations and how the standards can be adapted to meet a variety of contexts is reviewed. Finally, considerations for improving practice through ongoing evaluation by sport administrators and coach developers are discussed.

SECTION 1

Introduction

A sport coach is charged with creating a quality sport experience which guides the physical, technical, psychological, and social development of athletes on their team (Lyle & Cushion, 2017). Further, Côté and Gilbert (2009) noted that effective coaching is based on the application of professional, interpersonal, and intrapersonal knowledge within the sport context to further athlete development. As a person who contributes to the development of young people, the sport coach can play a critical role within society. However, quality experiences and positive development are not guaranteed without the sport coach engaging in formal, nonformal, and informal learning situations based on a body of knowledge specific to their profession. Given the societal relevance of coaching and the specialized knowledge needed to create quality sport experiences, there is an international and national movement occurring to promote the development of sport coaching (e.g., International Council for Coaching Excellence; United States Center for Coaching Excellence). While the development of coaching is multifaceted, one area of development required is the refining and researching of the core body of knowledge needed to be a competent sport coach. In fact, over 100 sport organizations agreed that a professional knowledge base specific to coaching is key to developing coaching expertise (NASPE, 2006). Since 1995, the National Standards for Sport Coaches have provided guidance in this endeavor.

Role and Purpose of the Standards

The *National Standards for Sport Coaches* (*NSSC*) identify the core responsibilities of a sport coach along with corresponding standards which outline the knowledge and skills needed to provide a quality sport experience. The *NSSC* were developed and revised based on the latest scientific evidence, to provide all

stakeholders associated with sport coaching a general understanding of what we should expect coaches to know and do to support quality experiences in sport. Therefore, the purpose of the *NSSC* are varied and dependent upon the stakeholder as noted in **Table 1.1**.

While the *NSSC* reflect the fundamental actions that administrators, athletes, and the public can expect of sport coaches, it is important to recognize that differences in depth and breadth of the knowledge as well as skills can be expected based on the level of coach expertise (e.g., volunteer beginning coach versus high school coach), the sport, the coaching context (e.g., youth sport versus intercollegiate sport), the local community, and culture. Thus, the *NSSC* provide a broad framework that sport coaches and sport administrators will need to adjust and adapt to work within their context. This does not mean that a standard would not apply to a particular context. However, it is recognized that adaptability will be necessary and encouraged. Section 4 highlights ways that various sport administrators, coach educators, and coach developers may implement the standards to promote coach development connected with various contexts.

History of the National Standards for Sport Coaches

Sensing the need to enhance the quality of sport coaching in the United States of America (USA), the National Association for Sport and Physical Education (NASPE), a former association under the auspices of the Society of Health and Physical Educators

Table 1.1 How Stakeholders May Use the National Standards for Sport Coaches

Sport coaches	Sport coaches may use the *NSSC* to better understand their coaching role and identify areas to gain further competence.
Athletes and their families	Athletes and their families may use the *NSSC* to inform them of what quality coaching looks like in practice.
Sport administrators	Sport administrators may use the *NSSC* to: • direct professional development opportunities for coaches. • determine coaching qualifications and construct assessment for coaches (e.g., competency checklists). • further clarify the role of support staff in assisting coaches in meeting the standards.
Coach educators	Coach educators may use the *NSSC* to construct curriculum for the education of sport coaches.
Coach developers	Coach developers may use the *NSSC* to construct curriculum for the education of sport coaches. Coach developers may use the *NSSC* to direct professional development opportunities for coaches.
Researchers	Researchers may use the *NSSC* to research: • the applicability of the standards for within a variety of coaching contexts, • the effectiveness of the standards in providing quality sport experiences, and/or • effective ways to develop the knowledge, skills, and competencies of sport coaches to meet their core responsibilities.

(SHAPE America; formerly American Alliance for Health, Physical Education, Recreation and Dance) brought together experts in the field to discuss the state of sport coaching and develop ideas for improving its quality. One of the proposed initiatives was to outline standards of practice for coaches related to the knowledge and skills needed to create a quality sport experience. In 1995, the task force released the *National Standards for Athletic Coaches* containing 350 competencies meant to help coach educators prepare coaches. As NASPE recognized the need to keep the national standards current, a process was put in place to review and revise standards to represent the most current research in the field. Thus, another task force was developed and the standards were revised in 2006. This version was renamed the *National Standards for Sport Coaches* and contained roughly 200 benchmarks organized into 40 standards placed within eight domains. These standards were supported by over 100 sport organizations. Additionally, the standards have been used by several sport organizations to develop content for educating coaches and several organizations have sought external evaluation of their use of the standards in their educational programs through the National Committee for the Accreditation of Coaching Education (see Appendix B).

Third Edition of the National Standards for Sport Coaches

SHAPE America, in 2015, commissioned a third edition of the *NSSC*. The revision was undertaken by two task forces representing experts in coaching and coach education. The task forces were asked to review and update the standards based on the latest scientific research and best coaching practices, consider alignment with the International Sport Coaching Framework (ICCE, ASOIF, and Leeds Metropolitan University, 2013) and quality coaching frameworks (e.g., Lara-Bercial et al., 2017; USOC, 2017), clarify the purpose of the *NSSC*, and formulate a communication plan for SHAPE America to disseminate them widely across the USA coaching landscape. The revision process included multiple meetings over a 3-year period in which the task force members reviewed current scientific research in the field, sought feedback from other researchers, coaches, coach educators, and administrators through two public reviews and two conference presentations. During the revision process the standards were aligned to correspond to the core responsibilities of coaches rather than domains of content knowledge. The full revision process and data obtained from public reviews is detailed in Gano-Overway et al. (2020).

Summary of Major Changes

The newly revised *NSSC* are organized into seven core responsibilities of coaching to more closely align with the International Sport Coaching Framework (ICCE et al., 2013). The core responsibilities are visually depicted in **Figure 1.1** to represent how the core responsibilities work together to help coaches create quality sport experiences and promote athlete development.

Under each of the newly identified seven core responsibilities are corresponding standards that identify competencies. Each standard is briefly described, providing insight into knowledge and skills that could be developed to help coaches achieve the competency (see Section 2).

Like the second edition, this third edition focused on identifying what coaches should know and do to create quality sport experiences across all sports and contexts. Similar to the previous edition, the third edition also continued to refine, clarify, and simplify the standards for use by multiple stakeholders. Therefore, the standards were updated based on the latest scientific research and best practices in coaching. For instance, updates were made to include concepts of long-term athlete development and strategic decision-making. Additionally, standards were added related to building cultural competence, highlighting the need to promote an emotionally and psychologically safe environment, developing inclusive practices, and considering coach self-care. To promote further streamlining, some of the standards were combined or clarified. For example, standards involving administrative tasks were tailored into a single standard and life skills development benchmarks consolidated into a distinct standard. Readers familiar with the previous edition will notice many similarities within the standards. To help those stakeholders who have relied on the second edition of the *NSSC* for program development, Appendix B shows the connections between the standards within each edition.

There are two major changes between the second and third editions. The first change is that the standards are now organized around the core responsibilities of sport coaching. The change represents an attempt to help coaches, athletes, and their families,

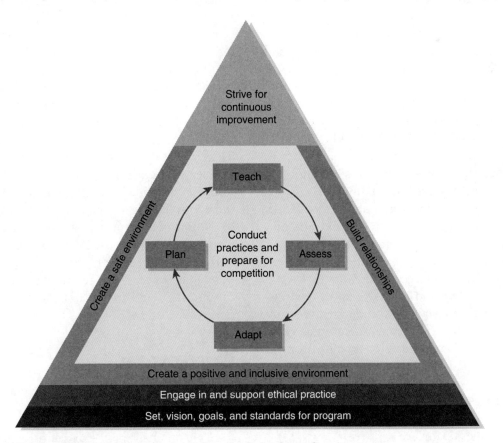

Figure 1.1 Core Responsibilities with the National Standards for Sport Coaches

Modified, with permission, from Gano-Overway, L., Van Mullem, P., Long, M., Thompson, M., Benham, B., Bolger, C., Driska, A., Moreno, A., & Schuster, D. (2020). Revising the National Standards for Sport Coaches within the USA, *International Sport Coaching Journal, 7*(1), 89–94. doi: 10.1123/iscj.2019-0058

and the general public clearly see the responsibilities coaches need to possess and enact to create quality sport experiences. These core responsibilities are listed here along with a brief description of how they connect to the previous domains.

- **Set vision, goals, and standards for sport program.** This core responsibility combined those standards that related to setting the vision for the program. Therefore, philosophy (Domain 1), long-term planning (Domain 4 & 5), and administrative (Domain 7) standards were re-oriented to focus on setting the vision, goals, and standards for the sport program.

- **Engage in and support ethical practice.** This core responsibility refocused the Philosophy and Ethics Domain 1 back to Ethics and re-emphasized for coaches and other stakeholders the importance of maintaining ethical standards within the sport context.

- **Build relationships.** This core responsibility highlights interpersonal knowledge and skills needed within the coaching profession to build positive relationships. This responsibility links to the standards in the Teaching and Communication Domain (Domain 5) and the Growth and Maturation Domain (Domain 4).

- **Develop a safe sport environment**. This core responsibility closely aligned with the Safety and Injury Prevention Domain (Domain 2). However, an emphasis was placed on developing an environment that was both physically and emotionally safe that moved beyond injury prevention. Therefore, standards related to health and safety, nutritional practices, and use of performance-enhancing drugs were incorporated into this responsibility. Additionally, creating an environment free of harassment and abuse was added. Finally, standards found in the Organization and Administration Domain (Domain 7) related to negligence and emergency action plans were streamlined under this core responsibility.

- **Create a positive and inclusive sport environment**. This core responsibility captured not only creating a positive environment that was a component of the Growth and Maturation Domain (Domain 4) and Teaching and Communication Domain (Domain 5), but also developing inclusive practices. Inclusive practices are now highlighted more clearly, beyond abiding by legal responsibilities (Domain 7).

- **Conduct practices and prepare for competition**. This core responsibility included many standards within the Physical Conditioning (Domain 3), Growth and Maturation (Domain 4), Teaching and Communication (Domain 5), Sport Skills and Tactics (Domain 6), and Evaluation (Domain 8) Domains. However, only those standards that directly related to conducting practices and preparing for competition were included around the main coaching actions of planning, teaching, assessing, and adapting.

- **Strive for continuous improvement**. This core responsibility built on some of the evaluative practices included the Evaluation Domain (Domain 8). However, it was broadened to emphasize the importance of reflection, lifelong learning, and self-care.

The second major change was the removal of the benchmarks in favor of providing a list of guiding topical references along with key resources and research references supporting each standard (see Section 3). This move was meant to provide coaches, program administrators, and coach educators/developers with topical references and resources to guide learning of knowledge and skills aligned with the standard without creating a rigid objective to be achieved. This was critical as the *NSSC* were created to provide guidance for coach development across levels of coach expertise (e.g., beginning to master coach), coaching contexts (e.g., recreational youth sport programs, interscholastic programs, etc.), and sports. The advantage of guiding topical references versus specific achievable benchmarks is that it gives learners as well as coach educators and coach developers flexibility for considering how best to meet the standards related to the coach's personal development and situational context. Therefore, it is hoped that outlining the general competencies within each standard and then providing resources to guide learning will allow all coaches and those responsible for guiding coach education and development to identify areas for continued improvement, regardless of coach expertise. To further assist in this endeavor, Section 5 reviews considerations for developing mastery by describing how stakeholders can use the standards for evaluation and assessment purposes.

Summary

The second edition of the *NSSC* ended with this statement:

> The optimal sport experience can only be brought about by caring and professionally trained coaches. Parents across the country send their children to practices and events

with the expectation that adult supervision will bring about positive sport outcomes and maximal learning and development. Athletes are willing to invest a great deal of time, money, and personal identity in developing their chosen sport skills. A system discourse of what coaches should know and do will advance all of our efforts in producing competent, qualified coaches. (NASPE, 2006, p. 6)

The third edition of the *NSSC* continues to embrace this sentiment and provides guidance to those interested in educating coaches in line with evidence-based coaching practices. The third edition also supports the profession of coaching by further delineating the specialized knowledge base needed to be an effective coach. Further, the third revision seeks to reach all stakeholders involved in sport. Thus, by identifying the core responsibilities of the *NSSC*,

athletes, their families, and the public will recognize the need for coaches to meet their coaching responsibilities at a level appropriate to their context prior to working with athletes. Finally, by identifying the general knowledge and skills underlying these core responsibilities, the *NSSC* provide coaches guidance on ways they can deepen their knowledge base within each of the 42 standards to improve their coaching practice over time.

While this newly revised edition builds upon the purpose of previous editions, it is recognized that this edition represents the current state of coaching practice. As further research is conducted and discourse occurs within the professional community, what represents competent coaching will evolve. Therefore, there is continued need for the *NSSC* to be updated regularly with new resources and evidence to share with all stakeholders.

REFERENCES

Côté, J., & Gilbert, W. (2009). An integrative definition of coaching effectiveness and expertise. *International Journal of Sports Science & Coaching, 4*, 307–323. doi: 10.1260/1747954 09789623892

Gano-Overway, L. A., Van Mullem. P., Long, M., Thompson, M., Benham, B., Bolger, C., Driska, A., Moreno, A., & Schuster, D. (2020). Revising the National Standards for Sport Coaches within the USA. *International Sport Coaching Journal, 7*, 89–94. doi: 10.1123/iscj.2019-0058

International Council for Coaching Excellence (ICCE), the Association of Summer Olympic Federations (ASOIF) and Leeds Metropolitan University (2013). *International sport coaching framework*. Human Kinetics.

Lara-Bercial, S., North, J., Hamalainen, K., Oltmanns, K., Minkhorst, J., & Petrovic, L. (2017). *European Sport Coaching Framework*. Human Kinetics.

Lyle, J., & Cushion, C. (2017). *Sport coaching concepts: A framework for coaching practice* (2nd ed.). Routledge.

National Association for Sport and Physical Education (NASPE) (2006). *Quality coaches, quality sports: National standards for sport coaches.* (2nd ed.). Author.

United States Olympic Committee (USOC). (2017). *Quality coaching framework*. Human Kinetics.

SECTION 2

National Standards for Sport Coaches

The *National Standards for Sport Coaches*, documented in this section, provide individuals with the seven core responsibilities of the coach. Under each of these core responsibilities are the competencies, identified as standards, that coaches should possess and continue to develop over the course of their career. The standards represent the knowledge, skills, and values that will help them to create a quality sport experience for their athletes.

Set Vision, Goals, and Standards for Sport Program

Sport coaches establish a clearly defined coaching philosophy and vision for their program. They develop, implement, and manage the goals for the program, in collaboration with sport program directors.
To meet this responsibility sport coaches:

Standard 1: *Develop and enact an athlete-centered coaching philosophy*

Focusing on the development of the whole athlete, sport coaches prioritize opportunities for development over winning at all costs. Sport coaches provide opportunities for athletes to reach their full potential within the sport.

Standard 2: *Use long-term athlete development with the intent to develop athletic potential, enhance physical literacy, and encourage lifelong physical activity*

Sport coaches understand and implement developmentally appropriate principles associated with long-term athlete development (e.g., American Development Model).

Standard 3: *Create a unified vision that corresponds to strategic planning and goal-setting principles*

Sport coaches create and implement goals important to the physical, behavioral, and social development of the athlete. The goals are aligned with the program vision, coaching philosophy, and long-term athlete development.

Standard 4: *Align program with all rules and regulations and needs of the community and individual athletes*

Sport coaches follow the applicable national, regional, local, and institutional rules and regulations to ensure the program is in compliance and eligible to compete. Sport coaches also align the program with the needs of the community and individual athletes.

Standard 5: *Manage program resources in a responsible manner*

Sport coaches manage program documents. They have a basic understanding of fiscal and facility management specific to their program. National Standards for Sport Coaches, SHAPE America, Retrieved from https://www.shapeamerica.org/uploads/pdfs/2018 /standards/National-Standards-for-Sport-Coaches -DRAFT.pdf

Engage in and Support Ethical Practices

Sport coaches understand the importance of ethical practices, engage in ethical behavior, abide by the codes of conduct affiliated with their sport and coaching context, and teach ethical behavior in their sport program.

To meet this responsibility sport coaches:

> **Standard 6:** *Abide by the code of conduct within their coaching context*

Sport coaches follow the code of conduct established by the governing bodies of the sport including international, national, regional, and/or local organizations.

> **Standard 7:** *Model, teach, and reinforce ethical behavior with program participants*

Sport coaches identify appropriate ethical behavior for their sport context and model it for their athletes. They make a deliberate attempt to teach and reinforce ethical behavior among their athletes.

> **Standard 8:** *Develop an ethical decision-making process based on ethical standards*

Sport coaches recognize the role of ethics in making decisions. They evaluate decision-making options using ethical approaches, determine the best course of action, and reflect upon their action to improve ethical decision-making in the future. National Standards for Sport Coaches, SHAPE America, Retrieved from https://www.shapeamerica.org/uploads/pdfs/2018/standards/National-Standards-for-Sport-Coaches-DRAFT.pdf

Build Relationships

Sport coaches develop competencies to effectively communicate, collaborate, educate, and support all stakeholders associated with the sport program (e.g., athletes, administrators, assistant coaches, support staff, referees, sports medicine professionals, program supporters, parents, media).

To meet this responsibility the sport coaches:

> **Standard 9:** *Acquire and utilize interpersonal and communication skills*

Sport coaches develop their interpersonal skills to build positive relationships with all stakeholders. These interpersonal skills include learning to engage in conversation, actively listening, understanding another's perspective, navigating personality styles, negotiating, maintaining self-control, and resolving conflicts. Sport coaches also make concerted efforts to develop positive coach-athlete relationships that are based on trust, commitment, clear expectations, appropriate interactions, constructive feedback, and support. Sport coaches work to develop their oral and written communication skills to concisely and clearly

communicate information, elicit community support, and advocate for the program.

> **Standard 10:** *Develop competencies to work with a diverse group of individuals*

Sport coaches develop sociocultural competencies to embrace and include diverse individuals (e.g., gender, race/ethnicity, religion, disability, sexual orientation, culture, socioeconomic status, etc.). These competencies include understanding how one's own background may affect how one interacts with others, understanding and appreciating others different from oneself, and appreciating how sociocultural norms, practices, and hierarchies in sport may influence stakeholders in positive and negative ways.

> **Standard 11:** *Demonstrate professionalism and leadership with all stakeholders*

Sport coaches cultivate their leadership skills in demonstrating professionalism with all stakeholders. They use leadership and management principles to help all stakeholders adopt the program vision, core values, and mission as well as encourage appropriate involvement. National Standards for Sport Coaches, SHAPE America, Retrieved from https://www.shapeamerica.org/uploads/pdfs/2018/standards/National-Standards-for-Sport-Coaches-DRAFT.pdf

Develop a Safe Sport Environment

Sport coaches create an emotionally and physically safe sport environment by following the practices outlined by sport organizations, coaching science, and state and federal laws.

To meet this responsibility sport coaches:

> **Standard 12:** *Create a respectful and safe environment which is free from harassment and abuse*

Sport coaches treat athletes and all program personnel with respect. They also use their personal and official power in a responsible manner to reduce the potential for abuse and sexual harassment. Sport coaches are proactive in preventing bullying and/or hazing behavior on the part of the athletes, staff, or spectators.

> **Standard 13:** *Collaborate with program directors to fulfill all legal responsibilities and risk management procedures associated with coaching*

Sport coaches understand the legal responsibilities of their position. Sport coaches identify and minimize potential risks based on sound risk management practices.

Standard 14: *Identify and mitigate physical, psychological, and sociocultural conditions that predispose athletes to injuries*

Sport coaches are aware of how health status, body structure, physical conditions, and periods of growth can predispose athletes to common injuries specific to the sport. Sport coaches are aware that an athlete's lack of sleep, fatigue, poor nutrition, and/or emotional state could warrant a change in practice plans to avoid injury.

Standard 15: *Monitor environmental conditions and modify participation as needed to ensure the health and safety of participants*

Sport coaches follow standards set forth by national safety organizations and/or local/state laws in regard to monitoring environmental conditions to modify or stop play and facilitate hydration. Sport coaches work with qualified sport medicine professionals to monitor environmental conditions such as heat, cold, or lightning.

Standard 16: *Reduce potential injuries by instituting safe and proper training principles and procedures*

Sport coaches implement safe training procedures. They ensure safe facilities and equipment, institute safe practice procedures, and supervise athletes during practice. Sport coaches recognize the biomechanical factors that underlie the causes of acute and chronic injuries relative to their sport and follow proper physiological training principles to avoid overtraining or injury.

Standard 17: *Develop awareness of common injuries in sport and provide immediate and appropriate care within scope of practice*

Sport coaches are trained in CPR/First Aid and concussion awareness and prevention. In response to an injury, sport coaches activate the emergency action plan. They also respond to the injury and/or refer an athlete to proper healthcare professionals.

Standard 18: *Support the decisions of sports medicine professionals to help athletes have a healthy return to participation following an injury*

Sport coaches work with sports medicine professionals to ensure a successful return to full participation following an injury. Sport coaches will provide a supportive environment that helps the injured athlete maintain social interactions during rehabilitation and addresses psychological issues with return to participation (e.g., self-confidence, motivation, fear of injury, etc.).

Standard 19: *Model and encourage nutritional practices that ensure the health and safety of athletes*

Sport coaches use sound nutritional practices (i.e., research-based, proven safe, and effective) with their athletes and in their own lives to promote a healthy lifestyle. They will promote dietary habits that fuel the athlete in a safe and healthy manner and encourage a healthy body image. Sport coaches are proactive in identifying potential eating disorders and referring athletes for appropriate professional assistance.

Standard 20: *Provide accurate information about drugs and supplements to athletes and advocate for drug-free sport participation*

Sport coaches are a reliable source of information about specific supplements/drugs by obtaining current, research-based information related to supplements/drugs and their potential impact on performance and health. Sport coaches will intervene and/or refer athletes to appropriate experts when significant changes in body composition, physical appearance, personality, and uncharacteristic behaviors that may be drug-related are observed. National Standards for Sport Coaches, SHAPE America, Retrieved from https://www.shapeamerica.org/uploads/pdfs/2018/standards/National-Standards-for-Sport-Coaches-DRAFT.pdf

Create a Positive and Inclusive Sport Environment

Sport coaches develop practices to maximize positive outcomes for their athletes by building season plans that promote physical, psychological, and social benefits for their athletes and encourage participation in sport. Sport coaches implement strategies to promote participation of all athletes.

To meet this responsibility sport coaches:

Standard 21: *Implement a positive and enjoyable sport climate based on best practices for psychosocial and motivational principles to maximize athlete and team well-being and performance*

Sport coaches create a positive sport climate by emphasizing effort and learning, encouraging athletes to keep winning in perspective, and promoting lifelong physical activity as an enjoyable endeavor. They help athletes learn from mistakes, improve their skills, and challenge their capabilities in an inviting and supportive environment. Sport coaches encourage athletes' personal responsibility and decision-making, build confidence, and create an environment where collectively the team can grow and work together toward a positive outcome for the team. Sport coaches promote athlete well-being and provide appropriate assistance and referral for mental health issues.

Standard 22: *Build inclusive practices into the program for all groups (e.g., race/ethnicity, gender/gender identity/ gender expression, religion, socioeconomic status, sexual orientation, nationality, etc.) which are aligned with current legal and ethical guidelines*

Sport coaches welcome all eligible athletes and implement strategies to encourage participation and value the contribution of underrepresented and disadvantaged groups. To effectively promote inclusivity, sport coaches follow legal (e.g., ADA, Title IX, etc.) and ethical guidelines to ensure that all athletes have equal opportunity to participate in athletics.

Standard 23: *Understand the importance of including athletes with disabilities in meaningful participation in established sport programs and consider options for athletes who cannot participate in traditional sport opportunities*

Sport coaches include athletes with disabilities with necessary accommodations that do not interfere with the integrity of the game or equal opportunities for all athletes, with and without disabilities, to be competitive. Sport coaches will work with administrators to provide appropriate alternatives if athletes with disabilities cannot participate in a traditional version of the sport. National Standards for Sport Coaches, SHAPE America, Retrieved from https://www.shapeamerica .org/uploads/pdfs/2018/standards/National-Standards -for-Sport-Coaches-DRAFT.pdf

Conduct Practices and Prepare for Competition

Sport coaches draw upon current coaching science, sport-specific knowledge, and best practices to conduct quality sport practices, prepare athletes for competition, and effectively manage contests. This practice can be framed around how coaches plan, teach, assess, and adapt in practices and competition. To meet this responsibility sport coaches:

Plan

Standard 24: *Create seasonal and/or annual plans that incorporate developmentally appropriate progressions for instructing sport-specific skills based on best practices in motor development, biomechanics, and motor learning*

Sport coaches structure plans that consider anticipated individual variability in physical, behavioral, and social maturity over the course of the season/year. Sport coaches plan for appropriate skill progressions based on the type of sport-specific skill and athletes' stages of learning, memory and attentional capabilities, motivation, etc.

Standard 25: *Design appropriate progressions for improving sport-specific physiological systems throughout all phases of the sport season using essential principles of exercise physiology and nutritional knowledge*

Sport coaches understand the basic principles and applications of training and program design. They are responsible for the physical training and conditioning that facilitates athlete development and performance. Although important to know these principles in relation to sport, it is also necessary to consider the principles holistically since many athletes are multi-sport athletes. Sport coaches design training programs and periodization plans that properly utilize physiological and biomechanical principles and implement nutritional guidelines for healthy eating to ensure optimal performance.

Standard 26: *Plan practices to incorporate appropriate competition strategies, tactics, and scouting information*

Sport coaches identify, develop, and apply competitive sport strategies and specific tactics appropriate for the age and skill levels of the participating athletes, unique characteristics of the competitive situation, and scouting information. Sport coaches involve athletes in selecting competitive strategies and seek to facilitate the strategic decision-making capabilities of all athletes.

Standard 27: *Incorporate mental skills into practice and competition to enhance performance and athlete well-being*

Sport coaches incorporate mental skills training at all age levels as a means to increase learning and performance, but also as part of the holistic development of the athlete. They provide training for mental skills (e.g., goal-setting, arousal regulation, attentional control, imagery/visualization, self-talk) through a periodized model that allows athletes to progress in their development of these skills and peak at appropriate times during the season. Sport coaches help athletes develop a mental competition plan that includes pre-competition preparation, contingency plan for errors during competition, and managing stress.

Standard 28: *Create intentional strategies to develop life skills and promote their transfer to other life domains*

Sport coaches plan strategies to teach important life skills (e.g., teamwork, leadership, persistence, social and emotional skills). Sport coaches show athletes how life skills can be useful in life domains outside of sport to increase the likelihood that they will be learned, practiced, and developed.

Standard 29: *Understand the components of effective contest management*

Sport coaches understand the importance of preparing facilities for competition, securing licensed officials, and promoting and demonstrating positive behavior to all officials, coaches and spectators.

Teach

Standard 30: *Know the skills, elements of skill combinations and techniques, competition strategies and tactics, and the rules associated with the sport being coached*

Sport coaches possess a deep understanding of all aspects of their particular sport and are aware of the rules, techniques, and competition strategies and tactics of their sport.

Standard 31: *Develop and utilize pedagogical strategies in daily practices*

Sport coaches know and use a variety of pedagogical approaches and instructional methods to help athletes learn techniques and tactics (e.g., accurate and timely demonstrations, games-based learning, problem-solving activities). Sport coaches also diversify these instructional strategies based on the needs of their athletes.

Standard 32: *Craft daily practice plans based on sound teaching and learning principles to promote athlete development and optimize competitive performance*

Sport coaches create daily practice plans using practice plan guidelines (e.g., opening comments, warm-up, practice objectives, appropriate progression of skills and conditioning, cool down, closing comments, post-practice reflections) and teaching and learning principles (e.g., enhancing time on task, planning for complexity to appropriately challenge athletes, simulating competition situations, instituting behavioral management practices, pacing instructional cues, providing feedback contingent upon performance, checking for athlete understanding and comprehension, etc.).

Standard 33: *Use appropriate motivational techniques to enhance performance and athlete engagement during practices and competitions*

Sport coaches follow best practices in motivating athletes. They consider individual differences in motivation and the effects of intrinsic and extrinsic rewards. Sport coaches communicate in ways that maximize motivation by focusing on positive corrective instruction, using encouragement, emphasizing effort and improvement and other factors athletes can control.

Assess

Standard 34: *Implement appropriate strategies for evaluating athlete training, development, and performance*

Sport coaches evaluate athlete progress and performance to assist in making decisions about athlete training, development, and performance. Sport coaches will use evidence-based strategies and tools as well as athlete input to make decisions regarding: athlete selection, assignment of team roles, goal-setting and training plan development, daily evaluation of progress, and incorporation of technology in training.

Standard 35: *Engage athletes in a process of continuous self-assessment and reflection to foster responsibility for their own learning and development*

Sport coaches provide athletes with the tools to evaluate their progress and encourage them to take initiative to make improvements in their own development. Sport coaches teach athletes to self-assess in order to nurture autonomy, decision-making skills, and to learn from mistakes.

Adapt

Standard 36: *Adjust training and competition plans based on athlete needs and assessment practices*

Sport coaches adjust periodization/season plans based on athlete progression, physical and mental health, modification of goals, etc. Sport coaches also adjust skills and tactics based on success and areas needing improvement throughout the season.

Standard 37: *Use strategic decision-making skills to make adjustments, improvements, or change course throughout a competition*

Sport coaches make adjustments during competition considering factors like the underlying principles of strategy and tactics within the sport and the skills and patterns of play of the opponent. Sport coaches also maintain self-control and monitor stress levels to facilitate effective decision-making. National Standards for Sport Coaches, SHAPE America, Retrieved from https://www.shapeamerica.org/uploads/pdfs/2018 /standards/National-Standards-for-Sport-Coaches -DRAFT.pdf

Strive for Continuous Improvement

Sport coaches continually improve through self-reflection, mentorship, professional development, evaluation, and self-care.

To meet this responsibility sport coaches:

Standard 38: *Regularly engage in self-reflection or peer-reflection to deeply examine situations, generate potential solutions, and think through those solutions*

Sport coaches take time to examine situations in greater depth by gathering insight from peer coaches and players and use these insights to improve coaching practice. Sport coaches will evaluate decision-making throughout the process and recognize that ambiguity exists, making regular reflection as well as systematic observations and guided trial and error important endeavors to improving coach practice.

Standard 39: *Develop an evaluation strategy to monitor and improve staff and team performance*

Sport coaches develop an evaluation strategy that fits with their seasonal demands, focus on continual improvement, and involve a range of stakeholders, such as players, coaching staff, administrators, support staff, and parents.

Standard 40: *Improve coaching effectiveness by seeking to learn the latest information on coaching through various avenues of coach development*

Sport coaches become continual learners. They take inventory of what they know and what they need to learn through performance improvement plans and needs analyses. They seek to improve through a variety of professional development and continuing education activities. Sport coaches search for the latest information on coaching, including sport science research and practical coaching information.

Standard 41: *Engage in mentoring and communities of practice to promote a learning culture and continual improvement*

Sport coaches serve as mentors and continually seek new mentors in their ongoing development. Sport coaches seek communities of practice (circles of coaches discussing coaching issues and means for improvement) to help promote a learning culture and continual improvement.

Standard 42: *Maintain work–life harmony and practice self-care to manage stress and burnout*

Sport coaches develop strategies to manage the stress experienced in coaching and develop strategies to preserve work–life harmony. By being physically and mentally healthy, coaches can be the best for themselves, their athletes, and their social communities. National Standards for Sport Coaches, SHAPE America, Retrieved from https://www.shapeamerica.org/uploads /pdfs/2018/standards/National-Standards-for-Sport -Coaches-DRAFT.pdf

© Miodrag ignjatovic/E+/Getty Images.

SECTION 3

Topics and Resources Related to the Standards

The purpose of this section is to provide coach educators and coach developers with the knowledge, skill, and behavior topics (labelled highlighted topics) typically associated with each standard of the *National Standards for Sport Coaches (NSSC)*. For each standard, a statement of knowledge, skill, and behavior is provided. Further, key resources (labelled helpful resources) and supporting research (labelled supporting research) are identified to reinforce each standard. Finally, to encourage continued development, the section concludes with guidelines for finding additional resources.

Note: The knowledge, skill, and behavior statements are not intended to be all-inclusive, but rather examples of the application of the standard to practice.

Set Vision, Goals, and Standards for Sport Program

Standard 1: *Develop and enact an athlete-centered coaching philosophy*

Highlighted Topics

- Coaches understand the importance of athlete-centered coaching.
- Coaches use language and terminology that reinforce effort and improvement, while keeping winning in perspective relative to the context in which they coach.
- Coaches construct a coaching philosophy relative to the context in which they coach.
- Coaches adjust and revise coaching philosophy, as needed.

Helpful Resources

Jenkins, S. (2010). Coaching philosophy. In J. Lyle & C. Cushion (Eds.), *Sports coaching: Professionalisation and practice* (pp. 233–242). Elsevier.

United States Olympic and Paralympic Committee. (2017). *Quality coaching framework*. Human Kinetics. Retrieved from: https://www.teamusa.org/About-the-USOPC/Programs/Coaching-Education/Quality-Coaching-Framework

Van Mullem, P., & Brunner, D. (2013). Developing a successful coaching philosophy: A step-by-step approach. *Strategies, 26*(3), 29–34. doi: 10.1080/08924562.2013.779873

Supporting Research

Gould, D., Pierce, S., Cowburn, I. H. J., & Driska, A. (2017). How coaching philosophy drives coaching action: A case study of renowned wrestling coach J Robinson. *International Sport Coaching Journal, 4*(1), 13–37. doi: 10.1123/iscj.2016-0052

McGladrey, B. W., Murray, M., & Hannon, J. C. (2010). Developing and practicing an athlete-centered coaching philosophy. *YouthFirst: Journal of Youth Sports, 5,* 4–8.

Miller, G. A., Lutz, R., & Fredenburg, K. (2012). Outstanding high school coaches: Philosophies, views, and practices. *Journal of Physical Education, Recreation & Dance, 83*(2), 24–29. doi: 10.1080/07303084.2012.10598724

Standard 2: *Use long-term athlete development with the intent to develop athletic potential, enhance physical literacy, and encourage lifelong physical activity*

Highlighted Topics

- Coaches understand the principles of long-term athletic development.
- Coaches can construct practices to develop fundamental movement patterns so as to enhance physical literacy.

- Coaches can identify developmental milestones for the age of the athlete they are coaching and provide developmentally appropriate skill progressions and physical training associated with age and stage.
- Coaches are able to read individual differences in athletes.
- Coaches can describe the benefits of physical activity for both health and performance.

Helpful Resources

Balyi, I., Way, R., & Higgs, C. (2013). *Long-term athlete development*. Human Kinetics.

Lloyd, R. S., Cronin, J. B., Faigenbaum, A. D., Haff, G. G., Howard, R., Kraemer, W. J., Micheli, L. J., Myer, G. D., & Oliver, J. L. (2016). National Strength and Conditioning Association position statement on long-term athletic development. *Journal of Strength Conditioning Research, 30*(6), 1491–1509. doi: 10.1519/JSC.0000000000001387

Sport for Life. (n.d.). *Long-term developmental stages*. Retrieved from: https://sportforlife.ca/long-term-development/

United States Olympic & Paralympic Committee. (n.d.). *Athlete development model*. Retrieved from: https://www.teamusa.org/About-the-USOPC/Programs/Coaching-Education/American-Development-Model

Supporting Research

Granacher, U. Lesinski, M., Busch, D., Muelbauer, T., Prieske, O., Puta, C., Gollhofer, A., & Behm, D. (2016). Effects of resistance training in youth athletes on muscular fitness and athletic performance: A conceptual model for long-term athlete development. *Frontiers in Physiology, 7*, 1–14. doi: 10.3389/fphys.2016.00164

Lang, M., & Light, R. (2010). Interpreting and implementing the Long Term Athlete Development Model: English swimming coaches' views on the (swimming) LTAD in practice. *International Journal of Sports Science & Coaching, 5*(3), 389–402. doi: 10.1260/1747-9541.5.3.389

Stodden, D. F., Goodway, J. D., Langendorfer, S. J., Roberton, M., Rudisill, M. E., Garcia, C., & Garcia, L. E., (2008). A developmental perspective on the role of motor skill competence in physical activity: An emergent relationship. *Quest, 60*(2), 290–306. doi: 10.1080/00336297.2008.10483582

Standard 3: *Create a unified vision that corresponds to strategic planning and goal-setting principles*

Highlighted Topics

- Coaches can explain the connection of coaching strategies to the long-term goals for the athletes and program.
- Coaches use appropriate tools and resources for long-term planning.
- Coaches make training decisions based on current athlete needs while considering long-term goals.

Helpful Resources

Gould, D. (2015). Goal setting for peak performance. In J. Williams & V. Krane (Eds.), *Applied sport psychology: Personal growth and peak performance* (7th ed., pp. 188–206). McGraw Hill.

Hedstrom, R. (n.d.). *Leading with vision: Developing your coaching point of view*. Association of Applied Sport Psychology. Retrieved from: https://appliedsportpsych.org/resources/resources-for-coaches/leading-with-vision-developing-your-coaching-point-of-view/

Monsma, E.V. (n.d.). *Principles of effective goal-setting*. Association of Applied Sport Psychology. Retrieved from: https://appliedsportpsych.org/resources/resources-for-coaches/principles-of-effective-goal-setting/

Pomazak, R. (2019, April 15). *Building a program culture by design: Beliefs/behaviors/mission/vision*. USA Football. Retrieved from: https://blogs.usafootball.com/blog/7184/building-a-program-culture-by-design-beliefs-behaviors-mission-vision

Weinberg, R. (2010). Making goals effective: A primer for coaches. *Journal of Sport Psychology in Action, 1*(2), 57–65. doi: 10.1080/21520704.2010.513411

Supporting Research

Fletcher, D., & Arnold, R. (2011). A qualitative study of performance leadership and management in elite sport. *Journal of Applied Sport Psychology, 23*(2), 223–242. doi: 10.1080/10413200.2011.559184

Gillham, A., & Weiler, D. (2013). Goal setting with a college soccer team: What went right, and less-than-right. *Journal of Sport Psychology in Action, 4*(2), 97–108. doi: 10.1080/21520704.2013.764560

Newland, M., Dixon, M. A., & Green, B. C. (2013). Engaging children through sport: Examining the disconnect between program vision and implementation. *Journal of Physical Activity and Health, 10*(6), 805–812. doi: 10.1123/jpah.10.6.805

Standard 4: *Align program with all rules and regulations and needs of the community and individual athletes*

Highlighted Topics

- Coaches describe how their coaching goals connect to the mission and vision of their organization.
- Coaches adjust their approach in reference to the needs of the athlete and program.
- Coaches reflect on how the prevailing sport culture might influence their behaviors related to rules and regulations.

Helpful Resources

National Alliance for Youth Sport. (n.d.). *Recommendations for communities*. Retrieved from: https://www.nays.org/resources/nays-documents/recommendations-for-communities/

Schloder, M. E., & McGuire, R. T. (2007). Coaching athletes: A foundation for success. LA84 Foundation. Retrieved from: https://la84.org/wp-content/uploads/2016/09/LA84CoachingManual.pdf

Special Olympics. (n.d.). *Athlete-centered coaching guide*. Retrieved from:https://media.specialolympics.org/resources/sports-essentials/general/AthleteCentered_CoachingGuide.pdf

Supporting Research

Denison, J., Mills, J. P., & Konoval, T. (2015). Sports' disciplinary legacy and the challenge of "coaching differently." *Sport, Education, and Society, 22*(6), 776–783. doi: 10.1080/13573322.2015.1061986

Kochanek, J., & Erickson, K. (2019). Outside the lines: An exploratory study of high school sport head coaches' critical praxis. *Psychology of Sport and Exercise, 45*, 1–10. doi: 10.1016/j.psychsport.2019.101580

McMahon, J., & Zehntner, C. (2014). Shifting perspectives: Transitioning from coach centered to athlete centered. *Journal of Athlete Centered Coaching, 1*(2), 1–19.

Standard 5: *Manage program resources in a responsible manner*

Highlighted Topics

- Coaches describe the organizational processes for resource management (i.e., fiscal, facility, time).
- Coaches consistently monitor the resources for which they are responsible.

Helpful Resources

Hoffman, K. (2013, March 14). The athletic budget balancing act. *Coach & A.D. Magazine*. Retrieved from: https://coachad.com/articles/marchapril-2013-budget-balancing-act/

Hoffman, K. (2017, March 22). Four popular budgeting styles used in athletic programs. *Coach & A.D. Magazine*. Retrieved from: https://coachad.com/articles/four-popular-budgeting-styles-used-in-athletic-programs/

Martens, R. (2012). *Successful coaching* (4th ed.). Human Kinetics.

Road Runners Club of America. (n.d.). *Managing club finances*. Retrieved from: https://www.rrca.org/resources/club-directors/manage-your-club/managing-club-finances

Supporting Research

Ammon, R., Southall, R. M., & Nagel, M. S. (2010). *Sport facility management: Organizing events and mitigating risks* (2nd ed.). FIT.

Blackburn, M. L., Forsyth, E., Olson, J. R., & Whitehead, B. D. (2013). *NIAAA's guide to interscholastic athletic administration*. Human Kinetics.

El-Komsan, A. W. M. R., & El-Gebaly, T. O. A. (2010). Time management of the training process and its relationship to the quality of decision making to coaches of some individual and team sports. *World Journal of Sport Sciences, 3*, 90–99.

Fried, G., DeSchriver, T. D., & Mondello, M. (2013). *Sport finance* (3rd ed.). Human Kinetics.

Kelley, D. J. (2012). *Sports fundraising: Dynamic methods for schools, universities, and youth sport organizations*. Routledge.

Engage in and Support Ethical Practices

Standard 6: *Abide by the code of conduct within their coaching context*

Highlighted Topics

- Coaches can identify the elements of a code of conduct.
- Coaches communicate expectations for behavior.
- Coaches align coaching behaviors within the code of conduct.

Helpful Resources

International Coaching Federation. (n.d.). *Code of ethics*. Retrieved from: https://coachfederation.org/code-of-ethics

USA Karate. (n.d.). *United States Olympic Committee coaching code of ethics*. Retrieved from: https://www.teamusa.org/USA-Karate/Officials-and-Coaches/Coaches-Resources/USOC-Coaching-Ethics-Code

US Center for Safe Sport. (n.d.). *Training and educational services*. Retrieved from: https://uscenterforsafesport.org/training-and-education/training-and-education-services/

Supporting Research

Bolter, N. D., Kipp, L., & Johnson, T. (2018). Teaching sportsmanship in physical education and youth sport: Comparing perceptions of teachers with students and coaches with athletes. *Journal of Teaching in Physical Education, 37*(2), 209–217. doi: 10.1123/jtpe.2017-0038

Jordan, J. S., Greenwell, T. C., Geist, A. L., Pastore, D. L., & Mahony, D. F. (2004). Coaches' perceptions of conference code of ethics. *Physical Educator, 61*(3), 131–145.

Schaefer, H. S., Yunker, C. A., Callina, K. S., Burkhard, B., Ryan, D., & Lerner, R. M. (2019). Indexing character in the context of sport participation within the United States Military Academy: The Character in Sport Index. *Journal of College and Character, 20*(4), 287–309. doi: 10.1080/2194587X.2019.1669464

Standard 7: *Model, teach, and reinforce ethical behavior with program participants*

Highlighted Topics

- Coaches can identify appropriate ethical boundaries in sport.
- Coaches use daily activities to teach ethical behavior.
- Coaches exhibit ethical coaching behaviors at all times.

Helpful Resources

Avelar Rosa, B. (2015, May). *Ethics in sport: Guidelines for coaches*. Retrieved from: http://www.pned.pt/media/31476/Ethics-in-Sport-Guidelines-for-Coaches.pdf

National Federation of State High School Associations. (n.d.). *Coaches code of ethics.* Retrieved from: https://www.nfhs.org/nfhs-for-you/coaches/coaches-code-of-ethics/

Simon, R. L. (Ed.). (2013). *The ethics of sport coaching: Moral, social, and legal issues* (4th ed). Westview Press.

True Sport. (n.d). *Teach.* Retrieved from: https://teach.truesport.org/

Supporting Research

Boardley, I. D., Kavussanu, M., & Ring, C. (2008). Athletes' perceptions of coaching effectiveness and athlete-related outcomes in rugby union: An investigation based on the coaching efficacy model. *The Sport Psychologist, 22*(3), 269–287. doi: 10.1123/tsp.22.3.269

Kassing, J. W., & Barber, A. M. (2007). Being a good sport: An investigation of sportsmanship messages provided by youth soccer parents, officials, and coaches. *Human Communication, 10*(1), 61–69.

Thompson, M., & Dieffenbach, K. (2016). Measuring professional ethics in coaching: Development of the PISC-Q. *Ethics and Behavior, 26*(6), 507–523. doi: 10.1080/10508422.2015.1060578

Yukhymenko-Lescroart, M. A., Brown, M. E., & Paskus, T. S. (2015). The relationship between ethical and abusive coaching behaviors and student-athlete well-being. *Sport, Exercise, and Performance Psychology, 4*(1), 36–49. doi: 10.1037spy0000023

Standard 8: *Develop an ethical decision-making process based on ethical standards*

Highlighted Topics

- Coaches are aware of models and/or tools to assist decision-making.
- Coaches can use multiple forms of reflection to process their decision-making.
- Coaches evaluate decisions thoroughly using a consistent set of ethical principles to guide the process.

Helpful Resources

Baghurst, T. M. & Parish, A. (2010). *Case studies in coaching: Dilemmas and ethics in competitive school sports.* Holcomb Hathaway.

Stoll, S. K., Van Mullem, H., Van Mullem, P., & Beller, J. M. (2017). The missing science: Ethics in practice. In M. Merc (Ed.), *Sport and Exercise Science.* IntechOpen: http://dx.doi.org/10.5772/intechopen.71883

Simon, R. L., Torres, C. R., & Hager, P. F. (2015). *Fair play: The ethics of sport.* Westview Press.

Thompson, M. (2019). Ethical and philosophical grounding of coaches. In K. Dieffenbach & M. Thompson (Eds.), *Coach education essentials* (pp. 17–34). Human Kinetics.

Supporting Research

Hardman, A., Jones, C., & Jones, R. (2010). Sports coaching, virtue ethics and emulation. *Physical Education and Sport Pedagogy, 15*(4), 345–359. doi: 10.1080/17408980903535784

Van Mullem, P., & Stoll, S. K. (2012). The impact of reflection on ethical decision making for sport leaders. *Journal of Contemporary Athletics, 6*(4), 233–241.

Build Relationships

Standard 9: *Acquire and utilize interpersonal and communication skills*

Highlighted Topics

- Coaches describe the principles of effective communication.
- Coaches employ active listening and effective communication strategies.
- Coaches use multiple communication styles when working with a variety of individuals.

Helpful Resources

Hanson, B. (n.d.). *Importance of communication in sports.* Athlete Assessments. Retrieved from: https://athleteassessments.com/importance-of-communication-in-sports/

Hedstrom, R. (n.d.). *Coaching through conflict: Effective communication strategies.* Association for Applied Sport Psychology. Retrieved from: https://appliedsportpsych.org/resources/resources-for-coaches/coaching-through-conflict-effective-communication-strategies/

Van Mullem, P., & Cole, M. (2015). Effective strategies for communicating with parents in sport. *Strategies: A Journal for Physical and Sport Educators, 28*(1), 13–17. doi: 10.1080/08924562.2014.980872

Supporting Research

Lorimer, R., & Jowett, S. (2013). Empathic understanding and accuracy in the coach-athlete relationship. In P. Potrac, W. Gilbert, & J. Denison (Eds.), *Routledge handbook of sports coaching* (pp. 321–332). Routledge.

Potrac, P., & Jones, R. (2011). Power in coaching. In R. Jones, P. Potrac, C. Cushion, & L. Tore Ronglan (Eds.), *The sociology of sports coaching.* London.

Rhind, D. J. A., & Jowett, S. (2010). Relationship maintenance strategies in the coach-athlete relationship: The development of the COMPASS model. *Journal of Applied Sport Psychology, 22*(1), 106–121. doi: 10.1080/10413200903474472

Smith, M. J., Figgins, S. G., Fewiss, M., & Kearney, P. E. (2018). Investigating inspirational leader communication in an elite team sport context. *International Journal of Sports Science & Coaching, 13*(2), 213–224. doi: 10.1177/1747954117727684

Smoll, F. L., Cumming, S. P., & Smith, R. E. (2011). Enhancing coach-parent relationships in youth sports: Increasing harmony and minimizing hassle. *International Journal of Sports Science & Coaching, 6*(1), 13–26. doi: 10.1260/1747-9541.6.1.13

Standard 10: *Develop competencies to work with a diverse group of individuals*

Highlighted Topics

- Coaches identify sociocultural factors that impact interpersonal relationships (e.g., gender, race/ethnicity, religion, disability, sexual orientation, culture, socioeconomic status, etc.).
- Coaches adjust coaching behaviors to accommodate a diverse population.
- Coaches demonstrate respect for all individuals involved in the program.

Helpful Resources

Cassidy, T., Jones, R., & Potrac, P. (2009). *Understanding sport coaching* (2nd ed.). Routledge.

NCAA (n.d.). *Office of inclusion.* Retrieved from: http://www.ncaa.org/about/resources/inclusion

Vealey, R. S., & Chase, M. A. (2016). Cultural competence in youth sport. In *Best practice for youth sport* (pp. 277–295). Human Kinetics.

USA Lacrosse. (n.d.). *Cultural competency.* Retrieved from: https://www.uslacrosse.org/diversity-inclusion/cultural-competency

Supporting Research

Nurden, J. W., & Lambie, G. W. (2011). Sociocultural competencies for sport coaches: A proposal for coaches and coach education. *Journal of Coaching Education, 4*(3), 3–29. doi: 10.1123/jce.4.3.3

Ryba, T. V., Stambulova, N. B., Si, G. & Schinke, R. J. (2013). ISSP Position Stand: Culturally competent research and practice in sport and exercise psychology. *International Journal of Sport and Exercise Psychology, 11*(2), 123–142. doi: 10.1080/1612197X.2013.779812

Tucker, C. M., Porter, T., Reinke, W. M., Herman, K. C., Ivery, P. D., Mack, C. E., & Jackson, E. S. (2005). Promoting teacher efficacy for working with culturally diverse students. *Preventing School Failure: Alternative Education for Children and Youth, 50*(1), 29–34. doi: 10.3200/PSFL.50.1.29-34

Standard 11: *Demonstrate professionalism and leadership with all stakeholders*

Highlighted Topics

- Coaches can describe their approach to leadership.
- Coaches adapt their leadership style to the professional setting.
- Coaches build relationships while maintaining appropriate professional behavior with all program participants.

Helpful Resources

Ehrmann, J. (2011). InSideOut coaching: How sports can transform lives. Simon & Schuster.

Gilbert, W. (2018, August 30). Coaching with an appropriate leadership style. *CoachesInsider.* Retrieved from: https://coachesinsider.com/track-x-country/articles-track-x-country/coaching-articles-track-x-country/coaching-with-an-appropriate-leadership-style-6/

National Collegiate Athletic Association. (n.d.). DiSC behavioral assessments. http://www.ncaa.org/disc-behavioral-assessments

Janssen, J., & Dale, G. (2002). *The seven secrets of successful coaches.* Winning the Mental Game.

Supporting Research

Brake, D. L. (2012). Going outside the lines of Title IX to keep coach-athlete relationships in bounds. *Marquette Sports Law Review, 22*(2), 395–426.

Arnold, R., Fletcher, D., & Molyneux, L. (2012). Performance leadership and management in elite sport: Recommendations, advice and suggestions from national performance directors. *European Sport Management Quarterly, 12*(4), 317–336.

Jowett, S., & Chaundy, V. (2004). An investigation into the impact of coach leadership and coach-athlete relationship on group cohesion. *Group Dynamics Theory, Research, and Practice, 8*(4), 302–311. doi: 10.1037/1089-2699.8.4.302

Turnnidge, J., & Côté, J. (2015). Applying transformational leadership theory to coaching research in youth sport: A systematic literature review. *International Journal of Sport and Exercise Psychology, 16*(3), 327–342. doi: 10.1080/1612197X.2016.1189948

Develop a Safe Sport Environment

Standard 12: *Create a respectful and safe environment which is free from harassment and abuse*

Highlighted Topics

- Coaches can describe key indicators of harassment and abuse in the sport setting.
- Coaches develop a set of referral resources for athletes.
- Coaches actively prevent bullying and hazing through athlete education and monitoring.
- Coaches reflect on how their position of power influences the coach-athlete relationship.

Helpful Resources

National Collegiate Athletic Association. (2016, September 26). *Addressing student-athlete hazing.* Retrieved from: http://www.ncaa.org/sport-science-institute/addressing-student-athlete-hazing

National Federation of State High School Associations. (2017, September 6). *Hazing in high school athletics.* Retrieved from: https://www.nfhs.org/articles/hazing-in-high-school-athletics/

US Center for Safe Sport (n.d.). *Parent toolkit.* Retrieved from: http://resources.safesport.org/toolkits/Parent-Toolkit-Complete/index.html

Supporting Research

Fasting, K., & Brackenridge, C. (2009). Coaches, sexual harassment and education. *Sport, Education and Society, 14*(1), 21–35. doi: 10.1080/1357332080802614950

Mountjoy et al. (2016). International Olympic Committee consensus statement: Harassment and abuse (non-accidental violence) in sport. *British Journal of Sports Medicine, 50*, 1–11. doi:10.1136/bjsports-2016-096121

Smittick, A. L., Miner, K. N., & Cunningham, G. B. (2019). The "I" in team: Coach incivility, coach gender, and team performance in women's basketball teams. *Sport Management Review, 22*(3), 419–433. doi: 10.1016/j.smr.2018.06.002

Steinfeldt, J. A., Vaughan, E. L., LaFollette, J. R., & Steinfeldt, M. C. (2012). Bullying among adolescent football players: Role of masculinity and moral atmosphere. *Psychology of Men & Masculinity, 13*(4), 340–353. doi: 10.1037/a0026645

Tomlinson, A., & Yorganci, I. (1997). Male coach/female athlete relations: Gender and power relations in competitive sport. *Journal of Sport and Social Issues, 21*(2), 134–155. doi: 10.1177/019372397021002003

Standard 13: *Collaborate with program directors to fulfill all legal responsibilities and risk management procedures associated with coaching*

Highlighted Topics

- Coaches can explain the legal responsibilities associated with their position.
- Coaches identify potential risks to self or athletes in their context.
- Coaches follow all policies and emergency action plans related to their position.

Helpful Resources

Andersen, J. C., Courson, R. W., Kleiner, D. M., & McLoda, T. A. (2020, March 9). National Athletic Trainer's Association position statement: Emergency planning in athletics. Retrieved from: https://www.ncbi.nlm.nih.gov/pmc/articles/PMC164314/pdf/attr_37_01_0099.pdf

Appenzeller, H. (2012). Risk management in sport: Issues and strategies (3rd ed.). Carolina Academic Press.

Figone, A. J. (2013). Seven major legal duties of a coach. *Journal of Physical Education, Recreation & Dance, 60*(7), 71–75. doi: 10.1080/07303084.1989.10606354

National Federation of State High School Associations (n.d.). *Fundamentals of Coaching.* Retrieved from: https://www.nfhs.org/media/1015481/fundamentals-of-coaching-manuscript.pdf

Supporting Research

Cotton, D. J., & Wolohan, J. T. (Eds.) (2017). *Law for recreation and sport managers* (7th ed.). Kendall Hunt Publishing.

Partington, N. (2017). Sports coaching and the law of negligence: Implications for coaching practice. *Sports Coaching Review, 6*(1), 36–56. doi:10.1080/21640629.2016.1180860

Singh, C., & Surujlal, J. (2010). Risk management practices of high school sport coaches and administrators. *South African Journal for Research in Sport, Physical Education and Recreation, 32*, 107–119.

Standard 14: *Identify and mitigate physical, psychological, and sociocultural conditions that predispose athletes to injuries*

Highlighted Topics

- Coaches can describe factors that increase an athlete's risk of injury.
- Coaches employ athlete monitoring strategies to inform practice planning.
- Coaches check in with athletes about their general health status.

Helpful Resources

American Academy of Pediatrics. (2017, March 16). *Sports injury prevention tips from the American Academy of Pediatrics.* Retrieved from: https://www.aap.org/en-us/about-the-aap/aap-press-room/news-features-and-safety-tips/Pages/Sports-Injury-Prevention-Tip-Sheet.aspx

Flegel, M. J. (2014). *Sport first aid.* Human Kinetics.

Johns Hopkins Medicine. (n.d.). *10 tips for preventing sports injuries in kids and teens.* Retrieved from: https://www.hopkinsmedicine.org/health/conditions-and-diseases/sports-injuries/10-tips-for-preventing-sports-injuries-in-kids-and-teens

Supporting Research

DiFiori, B., Benjamin, H. J., Brenner, J. S., Gregory, A., Jayanthi, N., Landry, G. L., & Luke, A. (2014). Overuse injuries and burnout in youth sport: A position statement from the American Medical Society for Sports Medicine. *British Journal of Sports Medicine, 48*(4), 287–288. doi: 10.1136/bjsports-2013-093299

Emery, A. (2003). Risk factors for injuries in child and adolescent sport: A systematic review. *Clinical Journal of Sport Medicine, 13*(4), 256–268. doi: 10.1097/00042752-200307000-00011

Fullagar, H. H., Skorski, S., Duffield, R., Hammes, D., Coutts, A. J., & Meyer, T. (2015). Sleep and athletic performance: The effects of sleep loss on exercise performance, and physiological and cognitive responses to exercise. *Sports Medicine, 45*(2), 161–186. doi: 10.1007/s40279-014-0260-0

Standard 15: *Monitor environmental conditions and modify participation as needed to ensure the health and safety of participants*

Highlighted Topics

- Coaches explain the risks of environmental conditions on athlete safety.
- Coaches are aware of the safety plans in place.
- Coaches modify behaviors (e.g., hydration practices) to account for environmental conditions.

Helpful Resources

Cappaert, T. A., Stone, J. A., Castellani, J. W., Krause, B. A., Smith, D., & Stephens, B. A. (2008). National Athletic Trainers' Association position statement: Environmental cold injuries. *Journal of Athletic Training, 43*(6), 640–658. doi: 10.4085/1062-6050-43.6.640

Casa, D. J., DeMartini, J. K., Bergeron, M. F., Csillan, D., Eichner, E. R., Lopez, R. M., Ferrara, M. S., Miller, K. C., O'Connor, F., Sawka, M. N., & Yeargin, S. W. (2015). National Athletic

Trainers' Association position statement: Exertional heat illness. *Journal of Athletic Training, 50*(9), 986–1000. doi: 10.4085/1062-6050-50.9.07

True Sport. (n.d.). *5 reasons why your athletes need a hydration plan.* Retrieved from: https://learn.truesport.org/why-athletes-need-hydration-plan/

USA Football. (n.d.). *Heat preparedness and hydration.* Retrieved from: https://usafootball.com/programs/heads-up-football/youth/heat-hydration/

Walsh, K. M., Cooper, M., Holle, R., Rakov, V., Roeder, W. P., & Ryan, M. (2013). National Athletic Trainers' Association position statement: Lightning safety for athletics and recreation. *Journal of Athletic Training, 48*(2), 258–270. doi: 10.4085/1062-6050-48.2.25

Supporting Research

Veneroso, C. E., Ramos, G. P., Mendes, T. T., & Simami-Garcia, E. (2015). Physical performance and environmental conditions: 2014 World Cup soccer and 2016 Summer Olympics in Brazil. *Temperature, 2*(4), 439–440. doi: 10.1080/23328940.2015.1106637

Thein, L. A. (1995). Environmental conditions affecting the athlete. *Journal of Orthopedic and Sport Physical Therapy, 21*(3), 158–171. doi: 10.2519/jospt.1995.21.3.158

Standard 16: *Reduce potential injuries by instituting safe and proper training principles and procedures*

Highlighted Topics

- Coaches can explain the basic impact of training on the body.
- Coaches plan progressions to allow for necessary physical adaptations.
- Coaches monitor athletes to ensure they are correctly performing skills to minimize the risk of injury.

Helpful Resources

Leonard, A. (n.d.). *Injury prevention and training periodization for high school and college athletes.* Retrieved from: https://www.witseducation.com/fit/news/industry/injury-prevention-training-periodization-high-school-college-athletes/

National Strength and Conditioning Association. (2020, March 9). *Athlete safety for strength coaches.* Retrieved from: https://www.nsca.com/education/athlete-safety/

Oates, W., & Barlow, C. (2011). An injury prevention curriculum for coaches. *Stop Sports Injuries.* Retrieved from: https://www.stopsportsinjuries.org//STOP/Downloads/Resources/CoachesCurriculumToolkit.pdf

Supporting Research

Côté, J., Lidor, R., & Hackfort, D. (2009). To sample or to specialize? Seven postulates about youth sport activities that lead to continued participation and elite performance. *International Journal of Sport and Exercise Psychology, 9*(1), 7–17. doi: 10.1080/1612197X.2009.9671889

Gamble, P. (2006). Periodization of training for team sports athletes. *Strength and Conditioning Journal, 28,* 56–66.

Lees, A. (2002). Technique analysis in sports: A critical review. *Journal of Sports Sciences, 20*(10), 813–828. doi: 10.1080/026404102320675657

Meeusen, R. et al. (2013). Prevention, diagnosis, and treatment of the overtraining syndrome: Joint consensus statement of the European College of Sport Science and the American College of Sports Medicine. *Medicine and Science in Sports and Exercise. 45*(1), 186–205. doi: 10.1249/MSS.0b013e318279a10a

Painter, K. B., Haff, G., Ramsey, M., McBride, J., Triplett, T., Sands, W., Lamont, H., Stone, M., & Stone, M. (2012). Strength gains: Block versus daily undulating periodization weight training among track and field athletes. *International Journal of Sports Physiology and Performance, 7*(2), 161–169. doi: 10.1123/ijspp.7.2.161

Standard 17: *Develop awareness of common injuries in sport and provide immediate and appropriate care within scope of practice*

Highlighted Topics

- Coaches explain common injuries affiliated with their sport.
- Coaches are Cardiopulmonary Resuscitation (CPR) and First Aid certified.
- Coaches implement emergency action plans, provide appropriate care, and refer when necessary.

Helpful Resources

American Red Cross. (n.d.). *First aid, health, and safety for coaches.* Retrieved from: https://www.redcross.org/take-a-class/cpr/wilderness-sports#sports-safety-training

National Federation of State High School Associations. (n.d.). *First aid, health, & safety.* Retrieved from: https://nfhslearn.com/courses/26/first-aid-health-and-safety

National Strength and Conditioning Association. (n.d.). *Athlete safety for strength coaches.* Retrieved from: https://www.nsca.com/education/athlete-safety/

Supporting Research

Broglio. S. P. Cantu, R. C., Gioia, G. A, Guskiewicz, K. M., Kutcher, J., Palm, M., & Valovich McLeod, T. C., (2014). National Athletic Trainers' Association position statement: Management of Sport Concussion. *Journal of Athletic Training, 49*(2), 245–265. doi: 10.4085/1062-6050-49.1.07

Drezner, J. A., Toreshahl, B. G., Rao, A. L., Hustzi, E., & Harmon, K. G. (2013). Outcomes from sudden cardiac arrest in US high schools: A 2-year prospective study from the National Registry for AED Use in Sports. *British Journal of Sports Medicine, 47*(18), 1179–1183. doi: 10.1136/bjsports-2013-092786

Johnson, S. T., Norcross, M. F., Bovbjerg, V. E., Hoffman, M. A., Change, E., & Koester, M. C. (2017). Sports-related emergency preparedness in Oregon high schools. *Sports Health: A Multidisciplinary Approach, 9*(2), 181–184. doi: 10.1177/1941738116686782

O'Donoghue, E. M., Onate, J. A., Van Lunen, B., & Peterson, C. L. (2009). Assessment of high school coaches' knowledge of sport-related concussions. *Athletic Training and Sports Health Care, 1*(3), 120–132. doi: 10.3928/19425864-20090427-07

Strand, B., David, S., Lymna, K. J., & Albrecht, J. M. (2017). Coaching in the United States: High school coaches' knowledge and confidence regarding athlete safety and injury management. *International Sport Coaching Journal, 4*(2), 220–234. doi: 10.1123/iscj.2016-0068

Whatman, C., Walters, S., & Shulter, P. (2018). Coach and player attitudes to injury in youth sport. *Physical Therapy in Sport, 32*, 1–6. doi: 10.1016/j.ptsp.2018.01.011

Standard 18: *Support the decisions of sports medicine professionals to help athletes have a healthy return to participation following an injury*

Highlighted Topics

- Coaches are aware of the limitations of the scope of practice of coaches.
- Coaches support each athlete on his or her journey following an injury.
- Coaches offer support and encouragement to athletes as they return to play.

Helpful Resources

American College of Sports Medicine; American Academy of Family Physicians; American Academy of Orthopaedic Surgeons; American Medical Society for Sports Medicine; American Orthopaedic Society for Sports Medicine; American Osteopathic Academy of Sports Medicine. (2002). The team physician and return-to-play issues: A consensus statement. *Medicine and Science in Sport and Exercise, 34*(7), 1212–1214. doi: 10.1097/00005768-200207000-00025

American College of Sports Medicine; American Academy of Family Physicians; American Academy of Orthopaedic Surgeons; American Medical Society for Sports Medicine; American Orthopaedic Society for Sports Medicine; American Osteopathic Academy of Sports Medicine. (2006). Psychological issues related to injury in athletes and the team physician: A consensus statement. *Medicine and Science in Sport and Exercise, 38*(11), 2030–2034. doi: 10.1249/mss.0b013e31802b37a6

Centers for Disease Control and Prevention. (2019, February 12). Returning to sports and activities. Retrieved from: https://www.cdc.gov/headsup/basics/return_to_sports.html

Weiss, W. (n.d.). *Mentally preparing athletes to return to play following injury.* Association for Applied Sport Psychology. Retrieved from: https://appliedsportpsych.org/resources/injury-rehabilitation/mentally-preparing-athletes-to-return-to-play-following-injury/

Supporting Research

Junge, A. (2000). The influence of psychological factors on sports injuries: Review of the literature. *American Journal of Sports Medicine, 28*(5 Suppl), 10–15.

May, K. H., Marshall, D. L., Burns, T. G., Popoli, D. M., & Polikandriotis, J. A. (2014). Pediatric sports specific return to play guidelines following concussion. *International Journal of Sports Physical Therapy, 9*(2), 242–255.

Podlog, L., & Dionigi, R. (2010). Coach strategies for addressing psychosocial challenges during the return to sport from injury. *Journal of Sport Sciences, 28*(11), 1197–1208. doi: 10.1080/02640414.2010.487873

Robbins, J. E., & Rosenfield, L. B. (2001). Athletes' perceptions of social support provided by their head coach, assistant coach, and athletic trainer, pre-injury and during rehabilitation. *Journal of Sport Behavior, 24*, 277–298.

Tenforde, A. S., & Fredericson, M. (2015). Athlete return-to-play decisions in sports medicine. *AMA Journal of Ethics, 17*(6), 511–514. doi: 10.1001/journalofethics.2015.17.6.ecas3-1506

Standard 19: *Model and encourage nutritional practices that ensure the health and safety of athletes*

Highlighted Topics

- Coaches describe nutritional demands of their sport.
- Coaches recognize the warning signs of disordered eating.
- Coaches promote healthy approaches to weight gain/maintenance/loss that are positive and safe and recommended by registered sport dieticians.

Helpful Resources

Alberta Health Services. (2018). Sports nutrition for youth: A handbook for coaches. Retrieved from: https://www.albertahealthservices.ca/assets/info/nutrition/if-nfs-sports-nutrition-for-youth.pdf

Bonci, L. (2009). *Sport nutrition for coaches.* Human Kinetics.

National Eating Disorders Association. (n.d.). *Coach and trainer toolkit.* Retrieved from: https://www.nationaleatingdisorders.org/sites/default/files/Toolkits/CoachandTrainerToolkit.pdf

True Sport. (n.d.). *Learn: Nutrition.* Retrieved from: https://www.teach.truesport.org/nutrition/

Supporting Research

Beckner, B. N., & Record, R. A. (2016). Navigating the thin-ideal in an athletic world: Influence of coach communication on female athletes' body image and health choices. *Health Communication, 31*(3), 364–373. doi: 10.1080/10410236.2014.957998

Desbrow, B., McCormack, J., Burke L. M., Cox, G. R., Fallon, K., Hislop, M., … & Star, A. (2014). Sports Dietitians Australia position statement: Sports nutrition for the adolescent athlete. *International Journal of Sport Nutrition and Exercise Metabolism, 24*(5), 570–584. doi: 10.1123/ijsnem.2014-0031

Jacob, R., Lamarche, B., Provencher, V., Laramee, C., Valois, P., Goulet, C., & Drapeau, V. (2016). Evaluation of a theory-based intervention aimed at improving coaches' recommendations on sports nutrition to their athletes. *Journal of the Academy of Nutrition and Dietetics, 116*(8), 1308–1315. doi: 10.1016/j.jand.2016.04.005

Martinsen, M., Sherman, R. T., Thompson, R. A., & Sundgot-Borgen, J. (2015). Coaches' knowledge and management of eating disorders: A randomized controlled trial. *Medicine & Science in Sports & Exercise, 47*(5), 1070–1078. doi: 10.1249/MSS.0000000000000489

Thomas, D. T., Erdman, K. A., & Burke, L. M. (2016). Position of the Academy of Nutrition and Dietetics, Dietitians of Canada, and the American College of Sports Medicine: Nutrition and athletic performance. *Journal of the Academy of Nutrition and Dietetics, 116*(3), 501–528. doi: 10.1016/j.jand .2015.12.006

Standard 20: *Provide accurate information about drugs and supplements to athletes and advocate for drug-free sport participation*

Highlighted Topics

- Coaches describe the current trends in supplement use.
- Coaches recognize significant changes in body composition that may be an indication of supplement use.
- Coaches use evidence-based resources to understand the impact of supplements on performance.
- Coaches educate athletes on the negative consequences of alcohol, tobacco, drugs, and banned substances.
- Coaches promote fair play and drug-free sport participation.

Helpful Resources

National Federation of State High School Associations (2015). *Dietary supplements position statement.* Retrieved from: https:// www.nfhs.org/media/1015652/dietary-supplements-position -statement-2015.pdf

True Sport. (n.d.). *Learn: Clean sport.* Retrieved from: https://www .teach.truesport.org/clean-sport/

World Anti-Doping Agency. (n.d.). *Resources.* Retrieved from: https://www.wada-ama.org

Supporting Research

Boardley, I. D., Grix, J., Ntoumanis, N., & Smith, A. L. (2019). A qualitative investigation of coaches' doping confrontation efficacy beliefs. *Psychology of Sport and Exercise, 45,* 101576.

Desbrow, B., McCormack, J., Burke L. M., Cox, G. R., Fallon, K., Hislop, M., Logan, R., Marino, N., Sawyer, S. M., Shaw, G., Star, A, Vidgen, H., & Leveritt. M. (2014). Sports Dietitians Australia position statement: Sports nutrition for the adolescent athlete. *International Journal of Sport Nutrition and Exercise Metabolism, 24*(5), 570–584. doi: 10.1123/ijsnem.2014-0031

Engelberg, T., Moston, S., & Blank, C. (2019). Coaches' awareness of doping practices and knowledge about anti-doping control systems in elite sport. *Drugs: Education, Prevention and Policy, 26*(1), 97–103. doi: 10.1080/09687637.2017.1337724

Thomas, D. T., Erdman, K. A., & Burke, L. M. (2016). Position of the Academy of Nutrition and Dietetics, Dietitians of Canada, and the American College of Sports Medicine: Nutrition and athletic performance. *Journal of the Academy of Nutrition and Dietetics, 116*(3), 501–528. doi: 10.1016/j.jand.2015.12.006

Create a Positive and Inclusive Sport Environment

Standard 21: *Implement a positive and enjoyable sport climate based on best practices for psychosocial and motivational principles to maximize athlete and team well-being and performance*

Highlighted Topics

- Coaches explain the principles of motivational climate and self-determination for individual athletes as well as the team.
- Coaches employ interpersonal skills to establish strong, safe relationships with athletes.
- Coaches use successes as an opportunity to build confidence in players.
- Coaches discuss failures as opportunities to learn and continue improving.
- Coaches assess team climate and, as a result, implement appropriate team-building strategies.

Helpful Resources

Fry, M. D., Gano-Overway, L. A., Guivernau, M., Kim, M., & Newton, M. (2020). *A coaches' guide to maximizing the youth sport experience: Work hard, Be kind.* Routledge.

National Collegiate Athletic Association. (n.d.). *Mental health resources.* Retrieved from: http://www.ncaa.org/sport-science -institute/mental-health-educational-resources

Nicholls, A. R. (2017). *Psychology in sports coaching* (2nd ed.). Routledge.

Positive Coaching Alliance. (n.d.) *PCA development zone resource center.* Retrieved from: https://devzone.positivecoach.org/

Supporting Research

Becker, A. (2009). It's not what they do, it's how they do it: Athlete experiences of great coaching. *International Journal of Sport Science & Coaching, 4*(1), 93–119. doi: 10.1260/1747 -9541.4.1.93

Côté, J., & Gilbert, W. (2009). An integrative definition of coaching effectiveness and expertise. *International Journal of Sport Science & Coaching, 4*(1), 307–323. doi: 10.1260/174795409789623892

Duda, J. L., & Appleton, P. R. (2016). Empowering and disempowering coaching climates: Conceptualization, measurement considerations, and intervention implications. In M. Raab, P. Wylleman, R. Seiler, A.-M. Elbe, & A. Hatzigeorgiadis (Eds.), *Sport and exercise psychology research: From theory to practice* (pp. 373–388). Elsevier Academic Press.

Ryan, R. M., & Deci, E. L. (2017). *Self-determination theory: Basic psychological needs in motivation, development, and wellness.* Guilford Press.

Standard 22: *Build inclusive practices into the program for all groups (e.g., race/ethnicity, gender/gender identity/gender expression, religion, socioeconomic status, sexual orientation, nationality, etc.) which are aligned with current legal and ethical guidelines*

Highlighted Topics

- Coaches can describe their own biases and how those might impact their coaching practice.
- Coaches modify practices and skill progressions as necessary to accommodate all athletes.
- Coaches work to eliminate barriers to sport participation related to race/ethnicity, gender/gender identity/gender expression, religion, socioeconomic status, sexual orientation, nationality, etc.

Helpful Resources

Burkett, B. (2013). Coaching athletes with a disability. In P. Potrac, W. Gilbert, & J. Denison (Eds.), *Routledge handbook of sports coaching* (pp. 196–209). Routledge.

Cotton, D. J., & Wolohan, J. T., (Eds.) (2017). *Law for recreation and sport managers* (7th ed.). Kendall Hunt Publishing.

National Collegiate Athletic Association. (2010, April). *Inclusion's best practices*. Retrieved from: https://www.ncaa.org/sites/default/files/InclusionsBestPractices.pdf

Supporting Research

Flores, M. M., Beyer, R., & Vargas, T. M. (2013). Making youth sport accessible to all athletes through coaching based on universal design for learning. *Journal of Youth Sports, 7,* 19–25. doi: 10.1260/1747-9541.10.5.783

Turnnidge, J., Vierimaa, M., & Côté, J. (2012). An in-depth investigation of a model sport program for athletes with a physical disability. *Psychology, 3*(12), 1131–1141. doi: 10.4236/psych.2012.312A167

Standard 23: *Understand the importance of including athletes with disabilities in meaningful participation in established sport programs and consider options for athletes who cannot participate in traditional sport opportunities*

Highlighted Topics

- Coaches describe accommodations that can be made to provide opportunities for participation for all athletes.
- Coaches can describe sport modifications that would not inhibit the integrity of the game and provide opportunity for competition for all athletes.
- Coaches work to create alternative sport experiences for athletes when necessary.

Helpful Resources

Beyer, R., Flores, M. M., & Vargas-Tonsing, T. M. (2009). Strategies and methods for coaching athletes with invisible disabilities in youth sport activities. *Journal of Youth Sports, 4*(2), 10–15.

Office for Civil Rights. (2015, January 25). *Students with disabilities in extracurricular activities.* Retrieved from: http://www.ed.gov/ocr/letters/colleague-201301-504.pdf

Special Olympics. (2013). *Athlete-centered coaching guide.* Retrieved from: https://media.specialolympics.org/resources/sports-essentials/general/AthleteCentered_Coaching Guide.pdf

Supporting Research

Martin, J. J., & Whalen, L. (2014). Effective practices of coaching disability sport. *European Journal of Adapted Physical Activity, 7*(2), 13–23.

Shapiro, D. R., & Martin, J. J. (2010). Athletic identity, affect, and peer relations in youth athletes with physical disabilities. *Disability and Health Journal, 3*(2), 79–85. doi: 10.1016/j.dhjo.2009.08.004

Wareham, Y., Burkett, B., Innes, P. & Lovell, G. P. (2017). Coaching athletes with disability: Preconceptions and reality. *Sport in Society: Cultures, Commerce, Media, Politics, 20*(9), 1185–1202. doi: 10.1080/17430437.2016.1269084

Conduct Practices and Prepare for Competition

Plan

Standard 24: *Create seasonal and/or annual plans that incorporate developmentally appropriate progressions for instructing sport-specific skills based on best practices in motor development, biomechanics, and motor learning*

Highlighted Topics

- Coaches describe general principles of the parent disciplines related to sport coaching (e.g., motor development, biomechanics, motor learning, psychology, etc.).
- Coaches plan practice sequences that are developmentally appropriate and maximize skill acquisition and retention.
- Coaches use athlete evaluations to refine the seasonal and annual plan.

Helpful Resources

Balyi, I., Way, R., & Higgs, C. (2013). *Long-term athlete development.* Human Kinetics.

Farrey, T., & Isard, R. (n.d.). *Physical literacy in the United States: A model, strategic plan, and call to action.* The Aspen Institute. Retrieved from: https://www.shapeamerica.org/uploads/pdfs/PhysicalLiteracy_AspenInstitute-FINAL.pdf

Gilbert, W. (2016). *Coaching better every season: A year-round system for athlete development and program success.* Human Kinetics.

Hooper, S. (2013). Planning and evaluating the program. In F. Pyke (Ed.), *Coaching excellence* (pp. 45–58). Human Kinetics.

Lloyd, R. S. Cronin, J. B., Faigenbaum, A. D., Haff, G. G., Howard, R., Kraemer, W. J., Micheli, L. J., Myer, G. D., & Oliver, J. L. (2016). National Strength and Conditioning Association position statement on long-term athletic development. *Journal of Strength Conditioning Research, 30*(6), 1491–1509. doi: 10.1519 /JSC.0000000000001387

United States Olympic and Paralympic Committee. (n.d.). *American development model.* Retrieved from: https://www .teamusa.org/About-the-USOPC/Programs/Coaching -Education/American-Development-Model

Supporting Research

Côté, J., Lidor, R., & Hackfort, D. (2009). To sample or to specialize? Seven postulates about youth sport activities that lead to continued participation and elite performance. *International Journal of Sport and Exercise Psychology, 9*(1), 7–17. doi: 10.1080/1612197X.2009.9671889

Hastie, P. A., & Wallhead, T. L. (2015). Operationalizing physical literacy through sport education. *Journal of Sport and Health Science, 4*(2), 132–138. doi: 10.1016/j.jshs.2015.04.001

Renshaw, I., Chow, J. Y., Davids, K., & Hammond, J. (2010). A constraints-led perspective to understanding skill acquisition and game play: A basis for integration of motor learning theory and physical education praxis? *Physical Education and Sport Pedagogy, 15*(2), 117–137. doi: 10.1080/17408980902791586

Stodden, D. F., Goodway, J. D., Langendorfer, S. J., Roberton, M., Rudisill, M. E., Garcia, C., & Garcia, L. E., et al. (2008). A developmental perspective on the role of motor skill competence in physical activity: An emergent relationship. *Quest, 60*(2), 290–306. doi: 10.1080/00336297.2008.10483582

Standard 25: *Design appropriate progressions for improving sport-specific physiological systems throughout all phases of the sport season using essential principles of exercise physiology and nutritional knowledge*

Highlighted Topics

- Coaches describe the physiological systems associated with sport participation.
- Coaches plan training programs that improve systems necessary for participation and competition at all phases of the season.
- Coaches encourage athletes to make nutritional choices that would fuel their training.

Helpful Resources

Hughes, M. G. (2007). Physiology for sports coaches. In R. L. Jones, M. Hughes, & K. Kingston (Eds.), *An introduction to sports coaching: From science to theory to practice* (pp. 126-137). Taylor & Francis.

Karpinksi, C., & Rosenbloom, C. A. (2017). *Sports nutrition: A handbook for professionals* (6th ed.). Academy of Nutrition and Dietetics.

National Strength & Conditioning Association (2015). *Essentials of strength training and conditioning* (4th ed.). Human Kinetics.

Thomas, D. T., Erdman, K. A., & Burke, L. M. (2016). American College of Sports Medicine joint position statement: Nutrition and athletic performance. *Medicine and Science in Sports and Exercise, 48*(3), 543–568. doi: 10.1249/MSS .0000000000000852

Supporting Research

Bailey, R., Collins, D., Ford, P., MacNamara, A., Toms, M., & Pearce, G. (2010). Participant development in sport: An academic review. *Sports Coach UK, 4,* 1–134.

Bergeron, M. F., Mountjoy, M., Armstrong, N., Chia, M., Côté, J., Emery, C. A., Faigenbaum A., Hall, G., Kriemler, S., Léglise, M., Malina, R. M., Pensgaard, A. M., Sanchez, A., Soligard, T., Sundgot-Borgen, J., van Mechelen, W., Weissensteiner, J. R., & Engebretsen, L. (2015). International Olympic Committee consensus statement on youth athletic development. *British Journal of Sports Medicine, 49*(13), 843–851. doi: 10.1136 /bjsports-2015-094962

Torres-McGehee, T. M., Pritchett, K. L., Zippel, D., Minton, D. M., Cellamare, A., & Sibilia, M. (2012). Sports nutrition knowledge among collegiate athletes, coaches, athletic trainers, and strength and conditioning specialists. *Journal of Athletic Training, 47*(2), 205–211. doi: 10.4085/1062-6050 -47.2.205

Standard 26: *Plan practices to incorporate appropriate competition strategies, tactics, and scouting information*

Highlighted Topics

- Coaches describe elements of practice plans and scouting reports.
- Coaches assess which sport tactics are appropriate for the athletes and situation in which they are coaching and include athletes in this process.
- Coaches use a variety of practice and competition strategies that are appropriate for the athletes and situation in which they are coaching.

Helpful Resources

Brown, B. (2020). *Youth coaching, four keys to a successful season.* Proactive Coaching. Retrieved from: https://proactivecoaching .info/shoppac/product/youth-coaching/

Hammermeister, J. J. (2010). *Cornerstones of coaching: The building blocks of success for sport coaches and teams.* Cooper.

Sabock, M. D., & Sabock, R. J. (2011). *Coaching: A realistic perspective* (10th ed.). Rowman & Littlefield.

Wrisberg, C. A. (2007). *Sports Skill Instruction for Coaches* (pp. 45–55). Human Kinetics.

Supporting Research

Côté, J., & Sedgwick, W. A. (2003). Effective behaviors of expert rowing coaches: A qualitative investigation of Canadian athletes and coaches. *International Sports Journal, 7,* 62–77.

DeMarco, Jr., G. M., & McCullick, B. A. (1997). Developing expertise in coaching: Learning from the legends. *Journal of Physical Education, Recreation & Dance, 68*(3), 37–41. doi: 10.1080/07303084.1997.10604909

Nash, C., Martindale, R., Collins, D., & Martindale, A. (2012). Parameterising expertise in coaching: Past present and future. *Journal of Sports Sciences, 30*(10), 985–994. doi: 10.1080/02640414.2012.682079

Standard 27: *Incorporate mental skills into practice and competition to enhance performance and athlete well-being*

Highlighted Topics

- Coaches describe the benefits of mental skills training at all levels of sport participation.
- Coaches determine the mental skills relevant for their sport and setting.
- Coaches implement a comprehensive mental skills training plan for all phases of the season.

Helpful Resources

Knight, C. J., Harwood, C. G., & Gould, D. (2018). *Sport psychology for young athletes.* Routledge.

Weinberg, R., & Butt, J. (2011). Building mental toughness. In D. Gucciardi & S. Gordon (Eds.), *Mental toughness in sport: Developments in theory and research* (pp. 212–229). Routledge.

Williams, J., & Krane, V. (2015). *Applied sport psychology: Personal growth and peak performance* (7th ed.). McGraw Hill.

Supporting Research

Gilbert, J. N., Gilbert, W., & Morawski, C. (2007). Coaching strategies for helping adolescent athletes cope with stress. *Journal of Physical Education, Recreation and Dance, 78*(2), 13–18. doi: 10.1080/07303084.2007.10597967

Schinke, R. J., & Jerome, W. C. (2002). Understanding and refining the resilience of elite athletes: An intervention strategy. *Athletic Insight: The Online Journal of Sport Psychology, 4*(3).

Thelwell, R. C., & Greenlees, I. A. (2003). Developing competitive endurance performance using mental skills training. *The Sport Psychologist, 17*(3), 318–337. doi: 10.1123/tsp.17.3.318

White, R. L., & Bennie, A. (2015). Resilience in youth sport: A qualitative investigation of gymnastics coach and athlete perceptions. *International Journal of Sports Science & Coaching, 10*, 379–393. doi: 10.1260/1747-9541.10.2-3.379

Standard 28: *Create intentional strategies to develop life skills and promote their transfer to other life domains*

Highlighted Topics

- Coaches discuss the life skills that can be learned through sport participation (e.g., teamwork, leadership, persistence, social, and emotional skills).
- Coaches intentionally discuss and promote life skills with athletes as they are being experienced in sport settings.
- Coaches discuss ways to transfer life skills learned in sport to other life domains with athletes.

Helpful Resources

Brown, B. (n.d.). *Life lessons for athletes.* Proactive Coaching. Retrieve from: https://proactivecoaching.info/shoppac/product/life-lessons-athletics/

Holt, N. L. (Ed.) (2016). *Positive youth development through sport* (2nd ed.). Routledge.

Hellison, D. (2011). *Teaching personal and social responsibility through physical activity* (3rd ed.). Human Kinetics.

Supporting Research

Blanton, J., Sturges, A. J., & Gould, D. (2014). Lessons learned from a leadership development club for high school athletes. *Journal of Sport Psychology in Action, 5*(1), 1–13. doi: 10.1080/21520704.2013.848827

Camiré, M., Trudel, P., & Bernard, D. (2013). A case study of a high school sport program designed to teach athletes life skills and values. *The Sport Psychologist, 27*(2), 188–200. doi: 10.1123/tsp.27.2.188

Pierce, S., Gould, D., & Camiré, M. (2017). Definition and model of life skills transfer. *International Review of Sport and Exercise Psychology, 10*(1), 186–211.

Price, M. & Weiss, M. R. (2013). Relationships among coach leadership, peer leadership, and adolescent athletes' psychosocial and team outcomes: A test of transformational leadership theory. *Journal of Applied Sport Psychology, 25*(2), 265–279. doi: 10.1080/10413200.2012.725703

Standard 29: *Understand components of effective contest management*

Highlighted Topics

- Coaches describe the logistical considerations for contest management (e.g., travel, accommodations, officials, facility preparation, etc.).
- Coaches employ organizational practices that keep all individuals informed of key competition information.
- Coaches promote and demonstrate respect for athletes, officials, and spectators.

Helpful Resources

Blackburn, M. L., Forsyth, E., Olson, J. R., & Whitehead, B. D. (2013). *NIAAA's guide to interscholastic athletic administration.* Human Kinetics.

Gilbert, W. (2016). *Coaching better every season: A year-round system for athlete development and program success.* Human Kinetics.

Martens, R. (2012). *Successful coaching* (4th ed.). Human Kinetics.

Supporting Research

Côté, J., Salmela, J. H., & Russell, S. (1995). The knowledge of high-performance gymnastic coaches: Competition and training considerations. *The Sport Psychologist, 9*(1), 76–95. doi: 10.1123/tsp.9.1.76

Washington, M., & Reade, I. (2013). Coach: The open system's manager. In P. Potrac, W. Gilbert, & J. Denison (Eds.) *Routledge handbook of sports coaching.* Routledge.

Teach

> **Standard 30:** *Know the skills, elements of skill combinations and techniques, competition strategies and tactics, and the rules associated with the sport being coached*

Highlighted Topics

- Coaches discuss the rules of the sport and associated skills and tactics.
- Coaches select strategies and tactics based on their athletes and competitors.
- Coaches maintain up-to-date knowledge of rules, skills, and tactics.

Helpful Resources

Gilbert, W., & Côté, J. (2013). Defining coaching effectiveness: Focus on coaches' knowledge. In P. Potrac, W. Gilbert, & J. Denison (Eds.) *Routledge handbook of sports coaching* (147–159). Routledge.

National Alliance for Youth Sport. (n.d.). *NAYS coach training and membership.* https://www.nays.org/coaches/

National Federation of State High School Associations. (n.d.). *NFHSLearn for you.* https://nfhslearn.com/

Supporting Research

de Souza, A., & Oslin, J. (2008). A player-centered approach to coaching. *Journal of Physical Education, Recreation, & Dance, 79*(6), 24–30. doi: 10.1080/07303084.2008.10598195

Pill, S. (2015). Using appreciative inquiry to explore Australian football coaches' experience with game sense coaching. *Sport, Education, and Society, 20*(6), 799–818. doi: 10.1080/13573322.2013.831343

> **Standard 31:** *Develop and utilize pedagogical strategies in daily practices*

Highlighted Topics

- Coaches explain the fundamentals of how people learn sport skills.
- Coaches employ a variety of evidence-based instructional strategies to maximize skill development.
- Coaches implement strategies to replicate game-like situations to facilitate tactics and decision-making.

Helpful Resources

Breed, R., & Spittle, M. (2011). *Developing game sense through tactical learning: A resource for teachers and coaches.* Cambridge University Press.

Mitchell, S., Oslin, J., & Griffin, L. (2013). *Teaching sport concepts and skills: A tactical games approach for ages 7 to 18* (3rd ed.). Human Kinetics.

Ong, N. T. & Hodges, N. J. (2012). Mixing it up a little: How to schedule observational practice. In N. Hodges & A. M. Williams (Eds.), *Skill acquisition in sport: Research, theory and practice* (2nd ed., pp. 22–39). Routledge.

Van Mullem, P., Shimon, J., & Van Mullem, H. (2017). Building a pedagogical coaching base: Pursuing expertise in teaching sport. *Strategies: A Journal for Physical and Sport Educators, 30*(5), 25–32. doi: 10.1080/08924562.2017.1344171

Wrisberg, C. A. (2007). *Sport skill instruction for coaches.* Human Kinetics.

Supporting Research

Dyson, B., Griffin, L. L., & Hastie, P. A. (2004). Sport education, tactical games, and cooperative learning: Theoretical and pedagogical considerations. *Quest, 56*(2), 226–240. doi: 10.1080/00336297.2004.10491823

Gallimore, R., & Tharp, R. G. (2004). What a coach can teach a teacher, 1975–2004: Reflection and reanalysis of John Wooden's teaching practices. *The Sport Psychologist, 18*(2), 119–137. doi: 10.1123/tsp.18.2.119

Light, R. (2004). Coaches' experiences of game sense: Opportunities and challenges. *Physical Education & Sport Pedagogy, 9*(2), 115–131. doi: 10.1080/1740898042000294949

Price, A., Collins, D. J., Stoszkowski, J. R., & Pill, S. (2019). Coaching games: Comparisons and contrasts. *International Sport Coaching Journal, 6*(1), 126–131. doi: 10.1123/iscj.2018-0015

> **Standard 32:** *Craft daily practice plans based on sound teaching and learning principles to promote athlete development and optimize competitive performance*

Highlighted Topics

- Coaches list the critical elements of a daily practice plan (e.g., opening comments, warm-up, practice objectives, appropriate progression of skills and conditioning, cool down, closing comments, post-practice reflections).
- Coaches consider how grouping athletes at practice (e.g., based on skill level, relationship, etc.) impacts the practice objectives.
- Coaches help athletes set meaningful goals to guide effort and attention during practice.
- Coaches maximize athlete development through delivery of appropriately-timed instructional cues.
- Coaches employ principles of effective feedback.

Helpful Resources

Coker, C. (2013). *Motor learning and control for practitioners.* Holcomb Hathaway Publishing.

Huber, J. J. (2013). *Applying educational psychology in coaching athletes.* Human Kinetics.

Kidman, L. (2011). Learning skill. In L. Kidman (Ed.), *The coaching process: A practical guide to becoming an effective sports coach* (3rd ed., pp. 123–144). Routledge.

Martens, R. (2012). *Successful coaching* (4th ed.). Human Kinetics.

Supporting Research

Denison, J. (2010). Planning, practice and performance: The discursive formation of coaches' knowledge. *Sport, Education and Society, 15*(4), 461–478. doi: 10.1080/13573322.2010.514740

Lara-Bercial, S., & Mallett, C. (2016). The practices and developmental pathways of professional and Olympic serial winning coaches. *International Sport Coaching Journal, 3*(3), 221–239. doi: 10.1123/iscj.2016-0083

Horn, T. S. (2019). Examining the impact of coaches' feedback patterns on the psychosocial well-being of youth sport athletes. *Kinesiology Review, 8*(3), 244–251. doi: 10.1123/kr.2019-0017

Standard 33: *Use appropriate motivational techniques to enhance performance and athlete engagement during practices and competitions*

Highlighted Topics

- Coaches describe multiple approaches to motivate athletes and how these might differ among individual athletes.
- Coaches identify the connection between coaching techniques and athlete motivation.
- Coaches recognize the signs of burnout and overtraining and make necessary adjustments to the environment.

Helpful Resources

Amorose, A. (2007). Coaching effectiveness: Exploring the relationship between coaching behavior and self-determined motivation. In M. S. Hagger & N. L. D. Chatzisarantis (Eds.), *Intrinsic motivation and self-determination in exercise and sport* (pp. 209–228). Human Kinetics.

Halden-Brown, S. (2003). *Mistakes worth making: How to turn sports errors into athletic excellence.* Human Kinetics.

Harwood, C., & Anderson, R. (2015). *Coaching psychological skills in youth football: Developing the 5Cs.* Bennion Kearney Limited.

Smith, R. E. (2015). A positive approach to coaching effectiveness and performance enhancement. In J. Williams & V. Krane (Eds.), *Applied sport psychology: Personal growth and peak performance* (7th ed., pp. 40 – 56). McGraw Hill.

Supporting Research

Adie, J. W., & Jowett, S. (2010). Meta-perceptions of the coach-athlete relationship, achievement goals, and intrinsic motivation among sport participants. *Journal of Applied Social Psychology, 40*(11), 2750–2773. doi: 10.1111/j.1559-1816.2010.00679.x

Feltz, D., Short, S., & Sullivan, P. (2008). *Self-Efficacy in sport: Research and strategies for working with athletes, teams, and coaches.* Human Kinetics.

Horn, T. S. (2008). Coaching effectiveness in the sport domain. In T. Horn (Ed.), *Advances in sport psychology* (pp. 239–268). Human Kinetics.

Keegan, R. J., Harwood, C. G., Spray, C. M., & Lavallee, D. E. (2009). A qualitative investigation exploring the motivational climate in early career sports participants: Coach, parent, and peer influences on sport motivation. *Psychology of Sport and Exercise, 10*(3), 361–372. doi: 10.1016/j.psychsport.2008.12.003

Lemyre, P. N., Treasure, D. C., & Roberts, G. C. (2006). Influence of variability in motivation and affect on elite athlete burnout susceptibility. *Journal of Sport and Exercise Psychology, 28*(1), 32–48. doi: 10.1123/jsep.28.1.32

Assess

Standard 34: *Implement appropriate strategies for evaluating athlete training, development, and performance*

Highlighted Topics

- Coaches discuss the evidence that would be required to make judgements about the effectiveness of tools used to evaluate athletes.
- Coaches incorporate technology as a means of monitoring athlete progress and health.
- Coach utilizes systematic observation tools to eliminate personal biases in the evaluation process.
- Coaches use positive communication strategies to communicate the results of evaluations with athletes.

Helpful Resources

Gilbert, W. (2016). *Coaching better every season: A year-round system for athlete development and program success.* Human Kinetics.

Groom, R., & Nelson, L. (2013). The application of video-based performance analysis in the coaching process: The coach supporting athlete learning. In P. Potrac, W. Gilbert, & J. Denison (Eds.), *Routledge handbook of sports coaching* (pp. 96–107). Routledge.

Hooper, S. (2013). Planning and evaluating the program. In F. Pyke (Ed.), *Coaching excellence* (pp. 45–58). Human Kinetics.

Supporting Research

Cope, E., Partington, M., & Harvey, S. (2017). A review of the use of a systematic observation method in coaching research between 1997 and 2016. *Journal of Sports Sciences, 35*(20), 2042–2050. doi: 10.1080/02640414.2016.1252463

Cushion, C. J., & Townsend, R. C. (2018). Technology-enhanced learning in coaching: A review of literature. *Educational Review, 71*(5), 631–649. doi; 10.1080/00131911.2018.1457010

Erickson, K., Côté, J., Hollenstein, T., & Deakin, J. (2011). Examining coach-athlete interactions using state space grids: An observation analysis in competitive youth sport. *Psychology of Sport and Exercise, 12*(6), 645–654. doi: 10.1016/j.psychsport.2011.06.006

Standard 35: *Engage athletes in a process of continuous self-assessment and reflection to foster responsibility for their own learning and development*

Highlighted Topics

- Coaches describe the benefits of including athletes in the assessment process.
- Coaches empower athletes to make informed training decisions and support those choices.
- Coaches include athletes in the process of evaluating coaching techniques in a nonpunitive manner.

Helpful Resources

Coker, C. (2018). *Motor learning and control for practitioners.* Routledge.

Gilbert, W. (2016). *Coaching better every season: A year-round system for athlete development and program success.* Human Kinetics.

Rynne, S. B., Crudgington, B., & Mallett, C. J. (2018). The coach as mentor. In R. Thelwell and M. Dicks (Eds.), *Professional advances in sports coaching: Research and practice* (pp. 228–247). Routledge.

Supporting Research

Chambers, K. L., & Vickers, J. N. (2006). Effects of bandwidth feedback and questioning on the performance of competitive swimmers. *The Sport Psychologist, 20*(2), 184–197. doi: /10.1123/tsp.20.2.184

Cleary, T. J., Zimmerman, B. J., & Keating, T. (2006). Training physical education students to self-regulate during basketball free throw practice. *Research Quarterly for Exercise and Sport, 77*(2), 251–262. doi: 10.1080/02701367.2006.10599358

Martindale, R. J., Collins, D., & Abraham, A. (2007). Effective talent development: The elite coach perspective in UK sport. *Journal of Applied Sport Psychology, 19*(2), 187–206. doi: 10.1080/10413200701188944

Adapt

Standard 36: *Adjust training and competition plans based on athlete needs and assessment practices*

Highlighted Topics

- Coaches explain how ongoing assessment impacts training adaptations.
- Coaches recognize indicators of athlete needs that supersede practice plans.
- Coaches engage in ongoing assessment and evaluation that results in training adaptations when necessary.

Helpful Resources

Hammermeister, J. J. (2010). *Cornerstones of coaching: The building blocks of success for sport coaches and teams.* Cooper.

Gilbert, W. (2016). *Coaching better every season: A year-round system for athlete development and program success.* Human Kinetics.

Sabock, M. D., & Sabock, R. J. (2011). *Coaching: A realistic perspective* (10th ed.). Rowman & Littlefield.

Wrisberg, C. A. (2007). Combining the practice of technical tactical and mental skills. In *Sports Skill Instruction for Coaches* (pp. 45–55). Human Kinetics.

Supporting Research

Gréhaigne, J., Bouthier, D., & Godbout, P. (1999). The foundations of tactics and strategy in team sports. *Journal of Teaching in Physical Education, 18*(2), 159–174. doi: 10.1123/jtpe.18.2.159

Jones, D. F., Housner, L. D., & Kornspan, A. S. (1997). Interactive decision making and behavior of experienced and inexperienced basketball coaches during practice. *Journal of Teaching in Physical Education, 16*(4), 454–468. doi: 10.1123/jtpe.16.4.454

Standard 37: *Use strategic decision-making skills to make adjustments, improvements, or change course throughout a competition*

Highlighted Topics

- Coaches explain how performance impacts selection of game strategy or tactics.
- Coaches recognize patterns in play and adjust tactics accordingly.
- Coaches incorporate strategies for emotion management to allow for effective decision-making.

Helpful Resources

Hammermeister, J. J. (2010). *Cornerstones of coaching: The building blocks of success for sport coaches and teams.* Cooper.

Sabock, M. D., & Sabock, R. J. (2011). *Coaching: A realistic perspective* (10th ed.). Lanham, MD: Rowman & Littlefield.

Supporting Research

Johnson, J. G. (2006). Cognitive modeling of decision making in sports. *Psychology of Sport and Exercise, 7*, 631–652. doi: 10.1016/j.psychsport.2006.03.009

Light, R. L., Harvey, S., & Mouchet, A. (2014). Improving "at-action" decision-making in team sports through a holistic coaching approach. *Sport, Education, and Society, 19*(3), 258–275. doi: 10.1080/13573322.2012.665803

Vergeer, I., & Lyle, J. (2009). Coaching experience: Examining its role in coaches' decision making. *International Journal of Sport and Exercise Psychology, 7*(4), 431–449. doi: 10.1080/1612197X.2009.9671918

Strive for Continuous Improvement

Standard 38: *Regularly engage in self-reflection or peer-reflection to deeply examine situations, generate potential solutions, and think through those solutions*

Highlighted Topics

- Coaches describe multiple approaches to self-reflection.
- Coaches engage in frequent reflective conversations with peers.

- Coaches employ objective reflective strategies (e.g., peer observation or video recording) to gain additional insight into one's practice.

Helpful Resources

McQuade, S. (2016, March 21). *Reflective practice is a key skill within coach development*. USA Football. Retrieved from:https://blogs.usafootball.com/blog/1496/reflective-practice-is-a-key-skill-within-coach-development

Mitchell, J. (2013, July 27). *Reflection as a coach development tool*. Coach Growth. Retrieved from: https://coachgrowth.wordpress.com/2013/07/27/reflection-as-a-coach-development-tool/

Cassidy, T., Jones, R., & Potrac, P. (2009). *Understanding sport coaching* (2nd ed.). Routledge.

Knowles, Z., Gilbourne, D., Cropley, B., & Dugdill, L. (Eds.), (2014). *Reflective practice in the sport and exercise sciences: Contemporary issues*. Routledge.

Supporting Research

Cushion, C. (2018). Reflection and reflective practice discourses in coaching: A critical analysis. *Sport, Education, and Society, 23*(1), 82–94. doi: 10.1080/13573322.2016.1142961

Gilbert, W. D., & Trudel, P. (2001). Learning to coach through experience: Reflection in model youth sport coaches. *Journal of Teaching in Physical Education, 21*(1), 16–34. doi: 10.1123/jtpe.21.1.16

Hall, E. T., & Gray, S. (2016). Reflecting on reflective practice: A coach's action research narratives. *Qualitative Research in Sport, Exercise, & Health, 8*(4), 365–379. doi: 10.1080/2159676X.2016.1160950

Koh, K. T., Mallett, C. J., Camiré, M., & Wang, C. K. J. (2015). A guided reflection intervention for high performance basketball coaches. *International Sport Coaching Journal, 2*(3), 273–284. doi: 10.1123/iscj.2014-0135

Kuklick, C., Gearity, B., & Thompson, M. (2015). The efficacy of reflective practice and coach education on intrapersonal knowledge in the higher education setting. *International Journal of Sports Science & Coaching, 9*(2), 23–42.

Taylor, S., Werthner, P., Culver, D., & Callary, B. (2015). The importance of reflection for coaches in parasport. *Reflective Practice, 16*(2), 269–284. doi: 10.1080/14623943.2015.1023274

Standard 39: *Develop an evaluation strategy to monitor and improve staff and team performance*

Highlighted Topics

- Coaches describe the importance of a multi-faceted evaluation process for all members of the coaching staff.
- Coaches incorporate strategies to elicit feedback from all stakeholders in a positive, nonthreatening manner.
- Coaches engage in mentoring of novice members of the coaching staff.

Helpful Resources

Gilbert, W. (2016). *Coaching better every season: A year-round system for athlete development and program success*. Human Kinetics.

Harris, B. S., Blom, L. C., & Visek, A. J. (2013). Assessment in youth sport: Practical issues and best practice guidelines. *Sport Psychologist, 27*(2), 201–211. doi: 10.1123/tsp.27.2.201

MacLean, J. (2001). *Performance appraisal for sport and recreation managers*. Human Kinetics.

Supporting Research

Cushion, C., Harvey, S., Muir, B., & Nelson, L. (2012). Developing the Coach Analysis and Intervention System (CAIS): Establishing validity and reliability of a computerised systematic observation instrument. *Journal of Sports Sciences, 30*(2), 201–216. doi: 10.1080/02640414.2011.635310

Ford, P., Coughlan, E., & Williams, M. (2009). The expert-performance approach as a framework for understanding and enhancing coaching performance, expertise and learning. *International Journal of Sports Science & Coaching, 4*(3), 451–463. doi: 10.1260/174795409789623919

Gillham, A., Dorsch, T., Walker, B., & Taylor, J. (2018). Coach, parent, and team assessments. In J. Taylor (Ed.), *Assessments for applied sport psychology consulting* (pp. 147–167). Human Kinetics.

Hoffmann, M. D., Duguay, A. M., Guerrero, M. D., Loughead, T. M., & Munroe-Chandler, K. J. (2017). 360-Degree feedback for sport coaches: A follow-up to O'Boyle. (2014). *International Sport Coaching Journal, 4*(3), 335–344. doi: 10.1123/iscj.2017-0063

Standard 40: *Improve coaching effectiveness by seeking to learn the latest information on coaching through various avenues of coach development*

Highlighted Topics

- Coaches identify the value in multiple coach development strategies (e.g., clinics, workshops, peer groups, webinars, self-study, etc.).
- Coaches are critical consumers of trends in sport to ensure they are utilizing evidence-based practices.
- Coaches adopt a systematic approach to planning for professional development.

Helpful Resources

Allison, W., Abraham, A., & Cale, A. (2016). *Advances in coach education and development*. Routledge.

Dieffenbach, K., & Thompson, M. (Ed.). (2019). *Coach education essentials*. Human Kinetics.

Sport New Zealand. (n.d.). *Coach development framework*. Retrieved from: https://sportnz.org.nz/assets/Uploads/attachments/managing-sport/coaching/Coach-Development-Framework.pdf

Supporting Research

Cushion, C. J., Armour, K. M., & Jones, R. L. (2003). Coach education and continuing professional development:

Experience and learning to coach. *Quest, 55*(3), 215–230. doi: 10.1080/00336297.2003.10491800

Mallett, C., Rynne, S., & Dickens, S. (2013). Developing high performance coaching craft through work and study. In P. Potrac, W. Gilbert, & J. Denison (Eds.), *Routledge handbook of sports coaching* (pp. 463–475). Routledge.

Nelson, L. J., Cushion, C. J., & Potrac, P. (2006). Formal, nonformal, and informal coach learning: A holistic conceptualisation. *International Journal of Sports Science & Coaching, 1*(3), 247–259. doi: 10.1260/174795406778604627

Wilson, L. M., Bloom, G. A., & Harvey, W. J. (2010). Sources of knowledge acquisition: perspectives of the high school teacher/coach. *Physical Education and Sport Pedagogy, 15*(4), 383–399. doi: 10.1080/17408980903273154

Standard 41: *Engage in mentoring and communities of practice to promote a learning culture and continual improvement*

Highlighted Topics

- Coaches describe what continued professional development resources are available to coaches.
- Coaches utilize opportunities to meet with peers to engage in shared learning experiences.
- Coaches seek formal and informal mentors across the span of their career.
- Coaches look for opportunities to mentor new coaches.

Helpful Resources

Bloom, G. (2013). Mentoring for sport coaches. In Potrac, P., Gilbert, W., & Denison, J. (Eds.), *Routledge handbook of sports coaching* (pp. 476–485). Routledge.

Cushion, C. (2015). Mentoring for success in sport coaching. In F. Chambers. (Ed.), *Mentoring in physical education and sports coaching* (pp. 155–162). Routledge.

Van Mullem, P., & Croft, C. (2018). Developing under the guidance of a mentor: Five strategies for coaches. *Strategies: A Journal for Physical and Sport Educators, 31*(6), 16–25. doi: 10.1080/08924562.2018.1515680

Van Mullem, P., & Croft, C. (2015). Planning your journey in coaching: Building a network for long-term success. *Strategies: A Journal for Physical and Sport Educators 28*(6), 15–22. doi: 10.1080/08924562.2015.1087903

Supporting Research

Bertram, R., Culver, D. M., & Gilbert, W. (2016). Creating value in a sport coach community of practice: A collaborative inquiry. *International Sport Coaching Journal, 3*(1), 2–16. doi: 10.1123/iscj.2014-0122

Garner, P., & Hill, D. M. (2017). Cultivating a community of practice to enable coach development in alpine ski coaches. *International Sport Coaching Journal, 4*(1), 63–75. doi: 10.1123/iscj.2016-0076

McQuade, S., Davis, L, & Nash, C. (2015). Positioning mentoring as a coach development tool: Recommendations

for future practice and research. *Quest, 67*(3), 317–329. doi: 10.1080/00336297.2015.1048810

Trudel, P., Culver, D. M., & Rynne, S. (2008). Clarifying the concept of communities of practice in sport: A response to commentaries. *International Journal of Sports Science & Coaching, 3*(1), 1–10. doi: 10.1260/174795408784089441

Rynne, S. B., Mallett, C., & Tinning, R. (2006). High performance sport coaching: Institutes of sport as sites for learning. *International Journal of Sports Science & Coaching, 1*(3), 223–234. doi: 10.1260/174795406778604582

Standard 42: *Maintain work-life harmony and practice self-care to manage stress and burnout*

Highlighted Topics

- Coaches describe the signs of stress and burnout.
- Coaches frequently engage in self-care practices (e.g., exercise, healthy eating, stress management, etc.).
- Coaches develop social support networks to offset the high demands of the profession.

Helpful Resources

Anderson, S. (n.d.). *#CoachToolKit: The importance of staying engaged and ignited.* Coaching Association of Canada. Retrieved from: https://coach.ca/coachtoolkit-importance-staying-engaged-and-ignited

Onate, J. (2016, October 5). Coaches' health: Keys for sleep, exercise, and mental health. National Federation for State High School Associations. Retrieved from: https://www.nfhs.org/articles/coaches-health-keys-for-sleep-exercise-and-mental-health/

United States Olympic and Paralympic Committee. (2017). *Quality coaching framework.* Human Kinetics. Retrieved from: https://www.teamusa.org/About-the-USOPC/Programs/Coaching-Education/Quality-Coaching-Framework

Supporting Research

Altfeld, S., Schaffran, P. Kleinert, J., & Kellmann, M. (2018). Minimising the risk of coach burnout: From research to practice. *International Sport Coaching Journal. 5*(1), 71–78. doi: 10.1123/iscj.2017-0033

Bopp, T., Wigley, B. J., & Eddosary, M. (2015). Job and life satisfaction: The perspective of collegiate head coaches. *International Journal of Sports Science & Coaching, 10*(6), 1025–1037. doi: 10.1260/1747-9541.10.6.1025

Bruening, J. E., & Dixon, M. A. (2007). Work-family conflict in coaching II: Managing role conflict. *Journal of Sport Management, 21*, 471–496.

Carson, F., Walsh, J., Main, L. C., & Kremer, P. (2017). High performance coaches' mental health and well-being: Applying areas of work life model. *International Sport Coaching Journal, 5*(3), 293–300. doi: 10.1123/iscj.2017-0078

Dixon, M. A., & Bruening, J. E. (2007). Work–family conflict in coaching I: A top-down perspective. *Journal of Sport Management, 21*, 377–406.

McNeill, K., Durand-Bush, N., & Lemyre, P. (2020). Can learning self-regulatory competencies through a guided intervention improve coaches' burnout symptoms and well-being? *Journal of Clinical Sport Psychology, 14*(2), 149–169. doi: 10.1123/jcsp.2018-0019

McNeill, K., Durand-Bush, N., & Lemyre, P. N. (2017). Understanding coach burnout and underlying emotions: A narrative approach. *Sports Coaching Review, 6*(2), 179–196. doi: 10.1080/21640629.2016.1163008

Guidelines for Finding Additional Resources

While the resources provided direct readers to references used to inform the creation of the *NSSC*, the list is by no means exhaustive. Sport stakeholders may wish to seek additional resources related to quality coaching. In the spirit of quality control, we offer the following suggestions for finding additional, credible resources:

- when possible, seek scientific research,
- look for resources that make reference to the research that supports the content,
- explore resources provided by national governing bodies rather than an individual coach,
- make note of the date of publication or update on resources to ensure the most current information,
- review author credentials for certifications, advanced education, etc., and
- attempt to align content with the *NSSC*.

SECTION 4

Apply the National Standards to Your Coach Development Context

Understanding the Role of Coach Developer

Anyone who supports coaches on their learning journey serves as a developer of coaches, including sport administrators, educators, and mentors. If an individual has specific training in designing, delivering, and facilitating coach education and development for coaches, they may also hold the title of coach developer. Thus, a coach developer is a person trained to support coaches in their ongoing professional development at all phases of their career (International Council for Coaching Excellence [ICCE], the Association of Summer Olympic Federations [ASOIF], & Leeds Metropolitan University, 2014). A coach developer must not only be an expert in their field but also understand the learning process and adult learners. Their roles include designing and evaluating educational programs, facilitating learning experiences for coaches, assessing coaches to encourage further professional development, and mentoring coaches. Therefore, coach developers customize coach development content to provide coaches with current information on coaching practice, share resources with coaches that may be applicable to coaching, serve as a trusted mentor on issues on which they seek advice, and engage in observation of and discussion with coaches to provide feedback to improve practice. Critical to completing these functions is an understanding of how coaches learn.

While there are currently very few individuals who are trained as coach developers, there are many individuals who perform some of the functions of a coach developer. For example, **coach educators** may design and evaluate educational programs, facilitate learning experiences, and mentor coaches. Additionally, **sport administrators** supervise coaches which includes facilitating learning experiences for coaches and assessing their development. Therefore, "coach developer" can also be seen as an umbrella term encompassing job duties of several occupations. In the remainder of this section, we highlight how all of these individuals, coach developers, coach educators, and sport administrators, can use the *National Standards for Sport Coaches (NSSC)* to inform how they complete the functions of a coach developer in their context. This begins with understanding learning settings and contexts.

Modes of Delivery and Learning

The development of coaching expertise is an ongoing process that takes place in a variety of formal, informal, and non-formal settings (ICCE, ASOIF, & Leeds Metropolitan University, 2014). In order to most effectively understand the coach development process, these settings must be understood. Formal coach development consists of highly structured programs that lead to degrees or certifications. These programs typically have well-defined expectations and performance metrics. Non-formal coach development might include less structured learning environments like clinics or workshops. Although these environments offer professional development, they generally have no assessment that determines the level to which the content impacted the participant. Informal learning in coaching typically happens through self-study or intentional reflection on one's daily work.

In addition to understanding the learning settings, it is also important to understand the context where coaches work and develop. The contexts described below are reflective of the most common coach development contexts in the United States.

- **Coaching associations**: Membership-based organizations that provides benefits to member coaches through coaching resources, professional development training, networking, and job placement. Example: *American Baseball Coaches Association.*
- **Higher education institutions:** Long-term coach education programs that are based in an academic setting. These programs range from a minor in an undergraduate program, full undergraduate majors, to master's degrees in sport coaching. The programs are typically multi-sport.
- **College/University athletic departments:** Public or private higher education institutions that provide support for intercollegiate athletic competition and provide professional development opportunities for coaches.
- **High school athletic departments:** Public or private schools that offer sport participation opportunities for adolescents (ages 13–18) and provide support for coaches.
- **State high school associations:** Organizations that coordinate the rules and regulations associated with high school competitions within a state. These include activities and sport programs. Many of these organizations also provide educational and development opportunities for sport coaches and administrators.
- **Multi-sport organizations:** Organizations that provide governance across sport in the educational setting in addition to coach education. Examples: *National Federation of State High School Associations or the National Collegiate Athletic Association.* Also, organizations that provide education to coaches across a wide range of sports and age levels. Example: *Positive Coaching Alliance (PCA) or National Alliance for Youth Sport (NAYS).*
- **National governing bodies (NGB):** Sport organizations that govern (e.g., rules, policies, sanctions,

etc.) a particular sport in a particular country and are designated by the United States Olympic and Paralympic Committee. The NGBs are often the source of education requirements for coaches in their sport participation pathway. Examples: *USA Hockey or USA Swimming.*
- **Youth Sport Organizations (Ages 6–14):** Public or private organizations that offer organized multisport or single-sport experiences for youth and provide educational opportunities for coaches.

While the list is not comprehensive, it is meant to act as a guide for examining how the standards might apply to the context in which coach developers may operate. The mode of delivery may also vary in each of these contexts. For example, institutions of higher education that offer degree programs in sport coaching might offer face-to-face, online courses, or a blend of the two. This is also true for NGBs that are preparing coaches in a face-to-face clinic or in an online learning platform. Regardless of the mode of delivery, curriculum designers for formal and non-formal settings must ensure that specific learning objectives have been identified and that the learning activities are appropriate to maximize the impact for learners. While a full review of adult learning principles is beyond the scope of this text, it should be noted that learning outcomes should drive curricular choices and that some type of assessment of those outcomes (beyond what the participants enjoyed) should drive future curricular choices. Coach developers, coach educators, and sport administrators are encouraged to review Sections 2 and 3 of this text to identify the learning objectives and learning experiences that represent the depth of knowledge and competence in the standards that will help them develop coaches based on their level of coaching expertise. Additionally, we recommend that coach developers, coach educators, and sport administrators review the remainder of this section to identify ways to use the *NSSC* to inform their coach developer functions within their context.

Applying the National Standards to Coach Developer Functions in a Variety of Contexts

As noted earlier, coach educators and sport administrators engage in a range of coach developer functions including designing educational programs, evaluating educational programs, providing resources important to coach functions, facilitating learning experiences, assessing coaches, and mentoring coaches. The remainder of this section outlines ways these functions could be informed by the *NSSC* within varying sport organizations. (*Note:* Rather than fully note standards or core responsibilities the core responsibility has been abbreviated and italicized within each example.)

Coaching Association Coach Educators/Developers

A coaching association serves member coaches and advocates on their behalf. Because a coaching association tends to be sport-specific, coach educators hired by the association or coach developers working in collaboration with the association can customize the education and development activities for the member coaches. Thus, the *NSSC* can serve as a guide in customizing content and curriculum for the coach developer working with or for the association. Coach educators and coach developers within coaching associations can use the *NSSC* in the following coach development activities:

Designing and Evaluating Coach Education Programs

- Design an online training module to reinforce the associations' code of conduct and help coaches to learn how to work with a diverse group of individuals and include inclusive practices. (*Set Vision & Goals / Create a Positive & Inclusive Environment*)
- Design an online training module to assess member coaches' understanding of how to role model positive behavior toward officials, coaches, and spectators. (*Engage in Ethical Practice*)
- Develop workshops that can be facilitated by a coach developer, on site, to assist coaches in recognizing their power to reduce the potential for abuse, sexual harassment, bullying, and/or hazing behavior. (*Develop a Safe Sport Environment*)
- Facilitate a coaching license program (if applicable) in best practices relative to the teaching of technical and tactical skills of the sport. (*Conduct Practices & Prepare for Competition*)

Providing Resources

- Share electronically, links to online resources on rule changes, return to play procedures, and the legal responsibilities of the coach. (*Develop a Safe Sport Environment*)
- Produce educational materials and distribute to member coaches on how coaches can manage

stress and maintain work–life harmony. (*Strive for Continuous Improvement*)

- Provide links on the coaching association website highlighting how coaches can complete CPR/First Aid and concussion awareness training. (*Develop a Safe Sport Environment*)
- Provide links to resources promoting sound nutritional practices and drug and supplement use among athletes. (*Develop a Safe Sport Environment*)
- Produce educational material on ADA guidelines and Title IX to promote inclusive practices and how to provide accommodations for athletes with disabilities. (*Create a Positive & Inclusive Environment*)
- Share electronically, links to online resources on long-term athlete development (LTAD). (*Set Vision & Goals*)

Facilitating Learning Experiences

- Conduct a workshop facilitated by a coach developer, on site, to teach appropriate ethical behavior and to develop the coach's ability to make ethical decisions. (*Engage in Ethical Practice*)
- Host an annual convention to provide knowledge base instruction on how coaches can adapt current methods to ever-changing athlete needs related to skill development, plan appropriate skill progression, evaluate athlete performance, and teach leadership and life skills. (*Conduct Practices & Prepare for Competition*)
- Host meet n' greet sessions at the annual convention to provide networking opportunities for coaches and help them build interpersonal skills. (*Strive for Continuous Improvement*)
- Invite member coaches to present at the annual convention to share methods for teaching strategies, techniques, and tactics associated with the sport. In addition, they can share information on best practices for planning practices, incorporating mental skills training, and motivational techniques to enhance athlete performance. (*Conduct Practices & Prepare for Competition*)

Assessing Coaches

- Design an assessment method to evaluate that best practices are being taught in current coach education programs in regard to safe and proper training procedures, risk management protocol, and injury response protocol. (*Develop a Safe Sport Environment*)
- Design self-assessment activities for member coaches to help them self-reflect on their ability to design seasonal/annual plans that include appropriate skill progression and the application

of appropriate training and conditioning principles. (*Strive for Continuous Improvement / Conduct Practices & Prepare for Competition*)

Evaluating Programs

- Offer member coaches assistance in assessing their sport program through self-reflection activities to improve their coaching performance and the performance of the staff and team. (*Strive for Continuous Improvement*)

Higher Education Institution Coach Educators/Developers

College and university academic programs specifically designed to prepare coaches are growing in numbers in the United States of America. While coach educators and coach developers have an advantage in these settings because they interact with the students over a 2- to 4-year period, there are also some disadvantages, like the power differential that comes with grading. Regardless, coach educators and coach developers within higher education institutions can use the *NSSC* in the following coach development activities:

Designing and Evaluating Coach Education Programs

- Map curriculum and content next to the *NSSC* to ensure all elements are addressed, considering the looping and progression of content as much as possible.
- Create course assignments that reflect the applied nature of the *NSSC* (e.g., writing practice plans in addition to testing knowledge of practice planning).
- Attempt to balance the curriculum with knowledge and applied experiences to encompass all *NSSC*.

Facilitating Learning Experiences

- Create practical opportunities that evolve in scope and intensity for each of the coaching behaviors in the *NSSC*.
- Help students explore their *Vision and Goals* for a sport program.
- Expose students to the coaching situations that might challenge them to *Engage in Ethical Practices*.
- Work with coaches to explore ways to implement a *Safe, Positive, and Inclusive Environment*.
- Support applied experiences that allow students to *Conduct Practices & Prepare for Competition* in their practices and competitive settings.

Assessing Coaches

- Allow for observation of the implementation of the *NSSC* in practice.
- Create evaluation tools based on the *NSSC*.

Mentoring Coaches

- Model the appropriate strategies to *Build Relationships* that will allow the coach developer to challenge ideas and behaviors.
- Teach reflection skills and support *Striving for Continuous Improvement* throughout practical/applied experiences.

College/University Athletic Department Sport Administrators/Coach Developers

In intercollegiate athletics, a coach is hired to provide leadership in managing the sport program, developing athletic skills, recruiting and retaining student-athletes, and achieving competitive success on the field of play. Because sport administrators in an intercollegiate athletic department are managing multiple sports, their role in providing coach education may be limited. In addition, a coach developer may be hired by the athletic department or individual teams to provide one-time or ongoing education for coaches. Thus, the *NSSC* can serve as a guide in customizing content and delivery methods for sport administrators and/or coach developers working with an athletic department. Specifically, sport administrators or coach developers can use the *NSSC* in the following coach development activities:

Designing and Evaluating Coach Education Programs

- Design an online educational module to inform coaches of the physical, psychological, and sociocultural conditions which predispose athletes to injury and how to reduce injuries through safe and proper training procedures. (*Develop a Safe Sport Environment*)
- Develop workshops to assist coaches in recognizing their power to reduce the potential for abuse, sexual harassment, bullying, and/or hazing behavior. (*Develop a Safe Sport Environment*)

Providing Resources

- Share electronically, links to online resources on the legal responsibilities of the coach and how to minimize risk in coaching practice. (*Develop a Safe Sport Environment*)

- Produce educational materials and distribute to the coaching staff on how coaches can manage stress and maintain work–life harmony. (*Strive for Continuous Improvement*)
- Provide links to the coaching staff through a weekly newsletter to promote resources on sound nutritional practices and updates on drug and supplement use among athletes. (*Develop a Safe Sport Environment*)
- Distribute educational material to the coaching staff on ADA guidelines and Title IX to promote inclusive practices and how to provide accommodations for athletes with disabilities. (*Create a Positive & Inclusive Environment*)
- Distribute informational material on injury response protocol and return to play procedures. (*Develop a Safe Sport Environment*)
- Provide web links to coaches through a weekly electronic message on how to develop an athlete-centered coaching philosophy and developmentally appropriate principles associated with long-term athlete development. (*Set Vision & Goals*)

Facilitating Learning Experiences

- Conduct a pre-season workshop for all members of the coaching staff to reinforce the department's code of conduct, any applicable rule changes in the intercollegiate sport setting, and to inform and teach fiscal and facility program management. (*Set Vision & Goals*)
- Offer a workshop to be implemented in the off-season, to teach appropriate ethical behavior, to develop the coach's ability to make ethical decisions, and help coaches learn how to work with a diverse group of individuals and include inclusive practices. (*Engage in Ethical Practice*)
- Host social gatherings and celebrations within the athletic department to provide networking and learning opportunities for coaches and help them build interpersonal skills. (*Strive for Continuous Improvement*)
- Organize internal coaching clinics and invite members of the coaching staff to share teaching strategies, best practices for planning practices, incorporating mental skills training, and motivational techniques to enhance athlete performance. (*Conduct Practices & Prepare for Competition*)
- Provide resources for coaches to participate in a coaching license program (if applicable) on best practices relative to the teaching of technical and tactical skills of the sport. (*Conduct Practices & Prepare for Competition*)

Assessing Coaches

- Design an assessment method to evaluate that best practices are being taught within each sport program in regard to safe and proper training procedures, risk management protocol, and injury response protocol. (*Develop a Safe Sport Environment*)
- Design self-assessment activities for member coaches to help them self-reflect on their ability to design seasonal/annual plans that include appropriate skill progression and the application of appropriate training and conditioning principles. (*Conduct Practices & Prepare for Competition*)
- Schedule two or more in-season meetings with each coach to provide feedback on the coach's ability to adapt current methods to ever-changing athlete needs related to skill development, plan appropriate skill progression, evaluate athlete performance, and teach leadership and life skills. (*Conduct Practices & Prepare for Competition*)

Mentoring Coaches

- Foster coach-to-coach interactions within the athletic department to nurture mentor-mentee relationships and help coaches cultivate leadership skills. (*Strive for Continuous Improvement*)
- Provide each member of the coaching staff with ongoing guidance on strategies for developing positive relationships with athletes and to build a positive team culture. (*Build Relationships*)
- Facilitate informal conversation with members of the coaching staff through "brown bag lunch" sessions to discuss topics such as building a positive culture and developing positive relationships. (*Create a Positive & Inclusive Environment*)

Evaluating Programs

- Offer head coaches assistance in assessing their sport program through self-reflection activities and evaluative tools to improve their coaching performance and the performance of the staff and team. (*Strive for Continuous Improvement*)

Interscholastic Athletic Department Sport Administrators

In interscholastic athletics, a coach is hired to provide leadership in managing the sport program, advancing athletes' physical, psychological, and social-emotional development, creating and providing a positive, safe, and risk-free learning environment, and achieving success in their programs. Because sport administrators in an interscholastic setting are managing multiple sports, their role in providing coaching education may be limited. However, sport administrators can still use the *NSSC* in the following coach development activities:

Providing Resources

- Distribute educational materials and distribute to the coaching staff on how coaches can manage stress and maintain work–life harmony. (*Strive for Continuous Improvement*)
- Provide web links to coaches through a weekly electronic message on how to develop an athlete-centered coaching philosophy and developmentally appropriate principles associated with long-term athlete development (LTAD). (*Set Vision & Goals*)

Facilitating Learning Experiences

- Implement a pre-season workshop for all members of the coaching staff (1) to share any applicable rule changes, (2) to inform and teach fiscal and facility program management, (3) to share injury response protocol, (4) to update return to play procedures, (5) to discuss the legal responsibilities of the coach, (6) to cover how to minimize risk, (7) to share ways to reduce the potential for abuse, sexual harassment, and bullying, and/or hazing behavior. (*Develop a Safe Sport Environment / Create a Positive & Inclusive Environment*)
- Implement a preseason workshop for all coaches on the (1) physical, psychological, and sociocultural conditions which predisposed athletes to injury, (2) how to reduce injuries through safe and proper training procedures, (3) sound nutritional practices, (4) drug and supplement use among athletes, (5) how to provide accommodations for athletes with disabilities, and (6) ADA guidelines and Title IX to promote inclusive practices. (*Develop a Safe Sport Environment / Create a Positive & Inclusive Environment*)
- Invite a local university coach educator to conduct a pre-service workshop to teach appropriate ethical behavior, to develop the coach's ability to make ethical decisions, and help coaches learn how to work with a diverse group of individuals and include inclusive practices. (*Engage in Ethical Practice*)
- Organize internal coaching clinics and invite members of the coaching staff to share teaching strategies, best practices for planning practices, incorporating mental skills training, and motivational techniques to enhance athlete performance. (*Conduct Practices & Prepare for Competition*)
- Provide funding for coaches to participate in a coaching license program (if applicable) on best practices relative to the teaching of technical and tactical skills of the sport. (*Conduct Practices & Prepare for Competition*)
- Provide resources for coaches to complete CPR/First Aid certification and/or attend national and regional coaching clinics to provide networking opportunities for coaches and help them build interpersonal skills. (*Strive for Continuous Improvement*)

Assessing Coaches

- Design self-assessment activities for member coaches to help them self-reflect on their ability to design seasonal/annual plans that include appropriate skill progression and the application of appropriate training and conditioning principles. (*Conduct Practices & Prepare for Competition*)
- Schedule two or more in-season meetings with coach to provide feedback on the coach's ability to adapt current methods to ever-changing athlete needs related to skill development, plan appropriate skill progression, evaluate athlete performance, and teach leadership and life skills. (*Conduct Practices & Prepare for Competition*)

Mentoring Coaches

- Foster coach-to-coach interactions within the athletic department to nurture mentor–mentee relationships and help coaches cultivate leadership and learning skills. (*Strive for Continuous Improvement*)
- Facilitate informal conversation with members of the coaching staff through "brown bag lunch" sessions to discuss topics such as building a positive culture and developing positive relationships. (*Conduct Practices & Prepare for Competition*)

Evaluating Programs

- Offer head coaches assistance in assessing their sport program through self-reflection activities to improve their coaching performance and the performance of the staff and team. (*Strive for Continuous Improvement*)
- Design end-of-season one-on-one evaluation sessions with the coach to evaluate the coach's fiscal and facility management ability as it relates to the program and to communicate the athletic department's athlete-centered coaching philosophy. (*Conduct Practices & Prepare for Competition*)

State High School Association Coach Educators

State High School Associations play a key role in ensuring coaches in the state provide quality sport experiences for student-athletes. The *NSSC* can assist

Association Directors and Coach Education Directors in this endeavor. The individual within state high school associations could support the work with coaches by using the *NSSC* in the following coach development activities:

Designing and Evaluating Educational Programs

- Align coach education programming offered by the state with the *NSSC* so state school coaches are clear regarding their core coaching responsibilities.
- When reviewing mandated educational programming for the state school coaches, make sure it is aligned with the *NSSC*.
- Use the *NSSC* as a guide to create educational resources (infographics, webinars, newsletters, web articles) for state coaches and/or sport administrators (i.e., activities/athletic directors).
- Evaluate current educational programming offered to state coaches to determine its effectiveness in helping coaches meet the core responsibilities outlined in the *NSSC*.
- Use the *NSSC* to determine how sport administrators and support staff can share the responsibilities (e.g., Can support staff be hired to manage facilities? Can sport administrators be tasked with developing protocols to assist coaches in evaluating and improving their programs?).

Facilitating Learning Experiences

- Develop a state-wide coaches conference that centers on the seven core responsibilities of coaching outlined in the *NSSC*. Invite exemplary coaches and coach education/coach developer experts from universities and colleges to share their implementation of the standards.

Assessing Coaches

- Develop a State High School Coaches Award based on criteria surrounding the *NSSC*.

Mentoring Coaches

- Share the *NSSC* with state sport administrators as it can provide ideas and resources for creating professional development programs, guidance for working with a struggling coach, and/or evaluating coach effectiveness beyond win/loss records.

Multi-Sport Independent Organization Coach Educators

Independent organizations that provide coach education across a variety of sports and competitive levels represent a unique approach to coach development in the USA. While some of these organizations focus on a narrow set of coach behaviors (e.g., *US Center for SafeSport*), others take a broad approach (e.g., *National Federation of State High School Associations*). The coach educators within multi-sport organizations can use the *NSSC* in the following coach development activities:

Designing and Evaluating Coach Education Programs

- Highlight all core responsibilities of coaches as indicated in the *NSSC*, even when the majority of the training is spent on one of these.
- Adapt the content and *NSSCs* to the specific context of the coaches, where possible.
- Use the *NSSC* as an evaluation tool to assess areas of deficiency in the curriculum.

Facilitating Learning Experiences

- Engage coaches in thought and discussion about the application of the *NSSC* core behaviors in their context via online learning experiences.
- Using web-based materials, ask coaches to discuss the similarities and differences in how they were coached with the standards for *Creating a Positive and Inclusive Sport Environment*.
- Provide checklists that allow coaches to review practice and competition plans and identify the elements that may need adjusting. (*Conduct Practices & Prepare for Competition*)

Assessing Coaches

- Assess coaches on their knowledge and application of *Developing a Safe Sport Environment*.
- Create assessment tools that align with both the *NSSC* and the course content.

Mentoring Coaches

- Create opportunities for participants to connect with one another that extend beyond the initial learning experiences.

National Governing Body Coach Educators/Coach Developers

National governing bodies (NGBs) provide significant influence in coach education and development in the United States. They are tasked with creating and implementing systems that can serve a large number of coaches to support the grassroots system, elite coaches to support high performance, and every level of coaching along the pathway. The *NSSC* can guide coach developers in NGBs in supporting coaches at every phase of their coaching career. The following are some suggestions for how the *NSSC* can be used when working with coaches in coach education systems across the NGB developmental pathway:

Designing and Evaluating Coach Education Programs

- Ensure that a system of coach development is in place that introduces the *NSSC* to coaches so all coaches are aware of their responsibilities.
- To promote the need to *Strive for Continuous Improvement*, design and implement a system of coach development that provides ongoing development for coaches that is in alignment with all areas of the *NSSC*.
- Design coach development curriculum with specific emphasis on *Engaging in Ethical Practices*.

Providing Resources

- Identify the appropriate *NSSC* in communication and educational materials developed for coaches.
- Use the *NSSC* as a tool for parents and league directors to promote quality coaching.

Facilitating Learning Experiences

- Provide learning experiences to regional and club directors on how to use the *NSSC* to educate and develop coaches.

Assessing Coaches

- Create an evaluation tool based on the *NSSC* to highlight areas of strength and areas for development to ensure coaches are developing holistically as they *Strive for Continuous Improvement*.
- Ask coaches at all levels to describe ways in which they implement the *NSSC* in their coaching to demonstrate the connection to all levels of coaching.

Mentoring Coaches

- Use the *NSSC* as a guide to help athletes in their transition into coaching roles.
- Allow high performance coaches to identify personal growth goals by reflecting on the *NSSC*.

Youth Sport Organizations (Paid Coaches) Sport Administrators

Within youth sport organizations there are many models for coaching. These models range from programs that rely exclusively on volunteer coaches to other programs that incorporate a system where master coaches work with volunteer coaches and pre-coaches. Here is one example of how a youth sport organization program director may implement the *NSSC* following a model for recognizing sport coaching as a profession and paying youth coaches a living wage allowing them

the time and support to make a difference in the lives of young people within communities. In this example, the program is a multi-sport year-round non-for-profit youth sport organization which has two directors (i.e., an executive director and a program administrator), six paid master coaches, and parent and previous program participant volunteer coaches (i.e., volunteer and pre-coaches). The program serves approximately 200 youth. The youth play three sports and stay with the same coaches throughout the year with volunteer coaches who assist with practices and at competitions. The program directors coordinate programming and provide coach education and opportunities for coach development. Outlined below are examples of how the administrators can work together to develop their coaches using the *NSSC* in the following coach development activities:

Providing Resources

- *Set Vision and Goals* aligned with an athlete-centered philosophy and considerations of long-term athlete development with coaches.
- Share the coaches' code of conduct for the program with coaches to *Support Ethical Practices*.
- Develop and share the emergency action plan for the facility with coaches to create a *Safe Sport Environment*.
- Establish and share policies, protocols, and cultural practices to ensure a *Safe Sport Environment* which is respectful and free from harassment and abuse.
- Make coaches aware of their legal responsibilities in order to *Develop a Safe Sport Environment*.
- Provide pamphlets for how to maintain a work–life harmony as well as a list of community resources for consultation to reduce stress and burnout to encourage *Striving for Continuous Improvement*.

Facilitating Learning Experiences

- Mandate all coaches complete a basic coach education course that aligns with all of the *NSSC* prior to coaching.
- Teach sport coaches how to develop positive coach–athlete relationships and develop competencies to work with diverse groups of individuals. (*Build Relationships*)
- Using a community of practice approach, provide a paid in-service day to have coaches meet to share their coaching practice. For example, coaches could share how they model, teach, and reinforce ethical behavior and make good ethical decisions in practice to *Engage in Ethical Practices*.

- Invite a sport dietician to educate coaches on general nutritional practices, healthy body image, eating disorders and supplements to *Develop a Safe Sport Environment.*
- Host a workshop on how to build inclusive practices into the program for all groups in accordance with *Create a Positive and Inclusive Sport Environment.*
- Help coaches *Conduct Practices and Prepare for Competition* by connecting coaches with online resources to learn how to teach the skills, elements of skill combinations and techniques, competition strategies and tactics, and the rules associated with the sports being coached.
- Conduct a practice learning session for all coaches to teach them ways to incorporate the games-based approach in their practices and provide effective demonstrations. (*Conduct Practices & Prepare for Competition*)

Assessing Coaches

- Assess coaches based on the *NSSC* through informal observations and evaluation tools. For example, observe coaches' strategies to help athletes learn from mistakes, improve their skills, and challenge their capabilities, and enjoy being active in an inviting and supportive environment and provide feedback for improvements aligned with *Create a Positive and Inclusive Sport Environment.*
- Have coaches share a practice plan and assess how the coach bases it on sound teaching and learning principles to promote athlete development and optimize performance. (*Conduct Practices and Prepare for Competitions*)

Mentoring Coaches

- Facilitate discussions with coaches to help them reflect on ways to improve their coaching practice aligned with *Strive for Continuous Improvement.*
- Help coaches create seasonal and/or annual plans that incorporate developmentally appropriate progressions for instructing sport-specific skills. (*Conduct Practices and Prepare for Competition*)
- Assist coaches in developing practice plans that will reduce potential injuries by instituting safe and proper training principles to *Develop a Safe Sport Environment.*
- Collaborate with coaches to identify which mental skills and life skills to focus on within program and identify intentional strategies to develop these skills during the season (*Conduct Practices and Prepare for Competition*)
- Work with coaches to develop plans for how to include athletes with disabilities in their sport programs to *Create a Positive and Inclusive Sport Environment.*
- Work with coaches to develop an appropriate tool to evaluate athlete development across the season. (*Conduct Practices and Prepare for Competition*)

Evaluating Program

- Working with coaches, identify and minimize potential risks based on sound risk management practices to *Develop a Safe Sport Environment.*
- Develop an evaluation strategy to monitor and improve staff and team performance to encourage *Striving for Continuous Improvement.*

Youth Sport Organizations (Volunteer Coaches) Sport Administrators

While it is not recommended to have an all-volunteer coaching staff, if program administrators choose to use this model, program administrators should take on a significant amount of the core responsibilities associated with the *NSSC* and provide coach education to cover the necessary competencies so that volunteer coaches can provide a positive sport experience for the youth athletes. In this example, the program administrator manages the program, ensures the sport environment and practice plans are developed and aligned with *NSSC*, educates coaches on their responsibilities during the coaching sessions, and monitors coaches to ensure they are effectively implementing the program according to program guidelines. Once trained, coaches just coach practices and competition based on predetermined plans provided by the administrator and are provided feedback on how to more effectively coach based on program guidelines. Therefore, all of the previously noted coach development strategies in the previous youth sport example apply except the program administrator is additionally developing resources and mentoring coaches to help achieve the program directives. Outlined below are some of the additional ways the sport administrator supports the coach by integrating the *NSSC* in the following coach development activities:

Providing Resources

- Administrators create an athlete-centered coaching philosophy and share with staff, coaches, athletes and their families and share ways that it is integrated into daily practice as noted in the core responsibility *Set Vision and Goals.*
- To further *Set Vision and Goals*, develop a long-term athlete development program aligned with

the American Development Model for their program that provides coaches a clear indication of what physical, psychological, and social-emotional development is planned at each level within the program.

- Design appropriate progressions within season, weekly, and daily plans for improving sport-specific physiological systems. (*Conduct Practices and Prepare for Competition*)
- Create daily practice plans for coaches aligned with *Developing a Safe Sport Environment* and *Conducting Practices and Preparing for Competition*.
- Establish procedures for team selection and assignment of team roles for the program. (*Conduct Practices and Prepare for Competition*)
- Develop athlete evaluation tools that coaches can use to assess athlete development over the course of the season as identified in *Conduct Practices and Prepare for Competition*.

Facilitating Learning Experiences

- As noted in the core responsibility of *Conduct Practices and Prepare for Competition*, teach coaches the skills, elements of skill combinations and techniques, competition strategies and tactics, and the rules associated with the sport being coached.

Mentoring Coaches

- Observe coaches to make sure the athlete-centered coaching philosophy is lived out during practices and competitions aligned with *Set Vision and Goals*.
- Observe coaches implementing practice plans and provide strategies for improving their coaching during the session related to giving effective demonstrations, planning for complexity to appropriately challenge athletes, instituting behavioral management practices, pacing instructional cues, providing feedback contingent upon performance, checking for athlete understanding and comprehension, etc. as noted in *Conduct Practices and Prepare for Competition*.
- Observe practices to see level of enjoyment and motivation exhibited by athletes and provide coaches appropriate motivational techniques to enhance performance and athlete engagement during practices, if needed. (*Conduct Practices and Prepare for Competition*)
- Working with the coaches, adjust training plans based on assessment and feedback from coaches and athletes as noted in *Conduct Practices and Prepare for Competition*.

REFERENCE

International Council for Coaching Excellence (ICCE), the Association of Summer Olympic Federations (ASOIF) and Leeds Metropolitan University. (2014). *International coach developers framework*. Human Kinetics.

SECTION 5

Resources for Promoting Quality Coaching

This section will offer considerations for encouraging quality coaching by providing the following three resources. First, sample job descriptions for a variety of contexts, including coaching duties and responsibilities framed around the *National Standards for Sport Coaches (NSSC)* are provided. Second, a table depicting what a coach should be able to do (i.e., knowledge/skills) along the pathways from beginning coach to striving for mastery relative to each standard is provided. Third, sample evaluation forms that offer examples of how an individual and/or organization charged with offering coach education can assess the ability and development of their coaches using the *NSSC*.

Job Descriptions

To assist sport administrators in hiring quality coaches, the following job descriptions offer examples of the responsibilities and qualifications of a coach in five different contexts using the *NSSC*.

- Sample A: Youth Sport Coach (see **Table 5.1**)
- Sample B: Head High School Coach (see **Table 5.2**)
- Sample C: Head Collegiate Coach (see **Table 5.3**)
- Sample D: Youth Performance Coach (see **Table 5.4**)
- Sample E: High Performance Coach (see **Table 5.5**)

Table 5.1 Sample Job Description A

Job Title: Youth Sport Coach

Job Description:
To provide instruction and leadership using the *National Standards for Sport Coaches* (*NSSC*) best practices in guiding youth (ages 6–14) including age-appropriate skill progression; athlete-centered coaching; a safe, positive, risk-free, and inclusive learning environment; and age-appropriate contest management.

Responsibilities*

- Use an athlete-centered coach philosophy (1) and model appropriate ethical behavior (7)
- Adhere to program rules and guidelines (4), and the organization's code of conduct (6)
- Create a safe sport environment and develop a culture free of harassment and abuse (12)
- Build inclusive practices into the program for all groups aligned with current legal and ethical guidelines (22, 23)
- Develop a positive climate by emphasizing effort and improvement, enjoyment, and learning from mistakes (21)
- Understand how to develop athletic potential, enhance physical literacy, and encourage lifelong physical activity through sport (2)
- Implement practice plans provided by administration that focuses on the technical skills of the sport (30) and is based on age-appropriate progression (24, 32)
- Teach sport specific skills, life skills, and competitive strategies relative to the organization's mission (4) and provide varied instructional techniques (31)
- Demonstrate self-control in competitive situations (37) and possess a willingness to improve coaching practice through the organization's training and coach education (40)

(continues)

Table 5.1 Sample Job Description A *(continued)*

- Identify potential risks associated with the sport (13, 15) and understand the appropriate protocol in responding to common injuries (17) and helping athletes "Return to Play" following an injury (18)

Qualifications

- Basic Coach Education Course
- CPR/First Aid Training
- Safe Sport Training
- Successful Completion of a Background Check

Preferred Qualifications

- Previous experience coaching youth sport
- Coursework and/or training relative to coaching youth

*Corresponding *NSSC* are represented by the numbers in ( ).

Table 5.2 Sample Job Description B

Job Title: Head High School Coach

Department/Group: School District

Job Description:

To provide instruction and leadership using the *National Standards for Sport Coaches* (*NSSC*), best practices to guide a high school athletic program including developing age-appropriate skill progression; enacting an athlete-centered coaching; engaging in ethical practice; creating a safe, positive, drug-free, and inclusive learning environment; conducting practices and preparing for competitions to promote athlete development; and engaging in ongoing professional development activities.

Responsibilities

- Use an athlete-centered coach philosophy (1) and a long-term development approach (2) in planning training procedures (25) and progression of skill development (24)
- Adhere to high school association rules (4) and the code of conduct (6)
- Model appropriate ethical behavior (7), manage program resources (5), demonstrate positive behavior to all officials, coaches, and spectators (29) in accordance with School District policies
- Create a safe sport environment and develop a culture free of harassment and abuse (12)
- Identify potential risks associated with the sport (13, 15) and/or participants (14) and adapt practice sessions accordingly (16)
- Promote sound nutritional practices (19), provide accurate information regarding drugs and supplement use, and advocate for a drug-free sport environment (20)
- Understand the appropriate protocol in responding to common injuries (17) and helping athletes "Return to Play" following an injury (18)
- Develop a positive and inclusive culture (10, 21) by emphasizing effort and learning (21), and by providing accommodations for athletes with disabilities (23)
- Plan instructional activities to develop mental skills (27), instill life skills (28), and incorporate age-appropriate competitive and tactical strategies (26)
- Teach sport-specific skills (30) and competitive strategies (32) using varied instructional (31) and motivational techniques (33)
- Implement a positive and enjoyable sport climate based on best practices (21)
- Build inclusive practices into the program for all groups (22)
- Understand components of effective contest management (29)
- Assess athlete (34) and program staff (39) performance and adapt planning and instruction accordingly (36)
- Demonstrate self-control in competitive situations (37) and a willingness to improve coaching practice through provided training and/or self-education (40–42)
- Engage in professional development activities (40–42) to improve interpersonal (9), intrapersonal (38), and professional (30) knowledge

Qualifications

- Basic Coach Education Course
- CPR/First Aid Certification & Concussion Training (17)
- Safe Sport Training (12)

- Successful Completion of a Background Check
- Previous experience coaching youth or interscholastic sport

Preferred Qualifications

- A Bachelor's Degree in Coaching or related degree
- 3 to 5 years of coaching experience
- National Certifications or Licensure relative to the sport being coached

*Corresponding *NSSC* are represented by the numbers in ( ).

Table 5.3 **Sample Job Description C**

Job Title: Head Collegiate Coach NCAA Institution

Department/Group: University Athletics

Job Description:

To provide leadership and management using the *National Standards for Sport Coaches* (*NSSC*), best practices to guide a collegiate athletic program including aligning with the university's mission and vision for athletics; managing program resources and personnel; adhering to ethical practice; cultivating relationships with all stakeholders; creating a safe, positive, drug free, and inclusive learning environment; conducting practices and preparing for competitions to promote athlete development; overseeing and evaluating program staff; conducting annual evaluations of program; and engaging in ongoing professional development activities.

Responsibilities

- Align program goals and objectives with the University's overall mission and vision for athletics (3)
- Adhere to NCAA rules (4) and the code of conduct (6)
- Develop a positive and inclusive culture (10, 21, 22) by emphasizing excellence through continuous improvement (21)
- Cultivate and develop relationships with all stakeholders (9) and demonstrate professionalism (11) when representing the University at all campus and off-campus functions
- Create season and practice plans that further develop technical skills, tactical skills, conditioning (30), and competitive strategies (32) using varied instructional methods (31)
- Possess good competitive and tactical decision-making skills and incorporate competitive and tactical strategies (26) for performance success
- Plan instructional activities to develop motivation (33) and mental skills (27) as well as instill life skills (28)
- Assess athlete (34) and program staff (39) performance and adapt planning and instruction accordingly (36)
- Demonstrate self-control in competitive situations (37) and a willingness to improve coaching practice through provided training and/or self-education (40–42)
- Model appropriate ethical behavior (7) and demonstrate positive behavior to all officials, coaches, and spectators (29) in accordance with NCAA guidelines
- Create a safe sport environment and develop a culture free of harassment and abuse (12)
- Identify potential risks associated with the sport (13, 15) and/or participants (14) and adapt practice sessions accordingly (16)
- Understand the appropriate protocol in responding to common injuries (17) and working with trained sport medicine professionals in "Return to Play" procedures following an injury (18)
- Promote sound nutritional practices (19), provide accurate information regarding drugs and supplement use, and advocate for a drug-free sport environment (20)
- Engage in professional development activities (40–42) to improve interpersonal (9), intrapersonal (38), and professional (30) knowledge
- Manage program fiscal and facility resources (5)

Qualifications

- A Master's Degree in Coaching or related field
- Prior collegiate coaching experience
- Successful Completion of a Background Check
- CPR/First Aid Certification and Concussion Training (17)
- Safe Sport Training (12)
- National Certifications or Licensure relative to the sport

Preferred Qualifications

- 3 to 5 years coaching collegiate athletes

*Corresponding *NSSC* are represented by the numbers in ( ).

Table 5.4 **Sample Job Description D**

Job Title: Youth Performance Coach

Job Description:
To provide instruction and leadership using the *National Standards for Sport Coaches* (*NSSC*) best practices to guide athletic development of youth (ages 6–18) including using long-term athlete development guidelines; adhering to the organization's code of conduct and professional ethics; creating a safe, positive, drug-free, and inclusive learning environment; conducting practices and preparing for competitions to promote athlete development; and engaging in ongoing professional development activities.

Responsibilities
- Use an athlete-centered coach philosophy (1) and a long-term development approach (2) in planning training procedures (25) and progression of skill development (24)
- Create a safe sport environment and develop a culture free of harassment and abuse (12)
- Develop a positive climate by emphasizing effort and improvement, enjoyment, and learning from mistakes (21)
- Build inclusive practices into the program for all groups (10, 22, 23)
- Adhere to the organization's code of conduct (6)
- Utilize interpersonal skills to build positive relationships with all stakeholders (9)
- Plan instructional activities to develop mental skills (27), instill life skills (28), and incorporate age-appropriate competitive and tactical strategies (26)
- Teach sport-specific skills (30) and competitive strategies (32) using varied instructional (31) and motivational techniques (33)
- Assess athlete performance (34) and adapt planning and instruction accordingly (36)
- Understand components of effective contest management (29)
- Demonstrate self-control in competitive situations (37) and a willingness to improve coaching practice through provided training and/or self-education (40–42)
- Model appropriate ethical behavior (7) and demonstrate positive behavior to all officials, coaches, and spectators (29) in accordance with the organization's policies
- Identify potential risks associated with the sport (13, 15) and/or participants (14) and adapt training sessions accordingly (16)
- Promote sound nutritional practices (19), provide accurate information regarding drugs and supplement use, and advocate for a drug-free sport environment (20)
- Understand the appropriate protocol in responding to common injuries (17) and helping athletes "Return to Play" following an injury (18)
- Engage in professional development activities (40–42) to improve interpersonal (9), intrapersonal (38), and professional (30) knowledge

Qualifications
- Prior coaching experience
- Successful Completion of a Background Check
- Safe Sport Training (12)
- CPR/First Aid Certification and Concussion Training (17)
- National Coaching Certifications or Licensure relative to teaching the sport and/or training performance athletes

Preferred Qualifications
- A Bachelor's Degree in Coaching or related field
- 3 to 5 years of experience training youth athletes

*Corresponding *NSSC* are represented by the numbers in ( ).

Table 5.5 **Sample Job Description E**

Job Title: High Performance Coach

Department/Group: National Governing Sport Organization

Job Description:
To provide instruction and leadership using the *National Standards for Sport Coaches* (*NSSC*), *Quality Coaching Framework*, and the *USOPC Coaching Principles* that identify best practices in guiding the development of athletes of all ages including the use of the American Development Model guidelines; adhering to the organization's

coaches code of conduct and professional ethics; creating a safe, positive, drug-free, and inclusive learning and developmental environment; conducting practices and preparing for competitions to promote athlete development; and engaging in ongoing professional development activities.

Responsibilities

- Align coaching goals and objectives with the organization's overall mission and visions for sport (3)
- Adhere to the organization's rules (4) and the code of conduct (6)
- Develop a positive and inclusive culture (10, 21, 22) by emphasizing excellence through continuous improvement (21)
- Create a safe sport environment and develop a culture free of harassment and abuse (12)
- Cultivate and develop relationships with all stakeholders (9) and demonstrate professionalism (11) when representing the organization
- Create season and practice plans that further develop technical skills, tactical skills, conditioning (30), and competitive strategies (32) using varied instructional methods (31)
- Plan instructional activities to develop motivation (33) and mental skills (27) as well as instill life skills (28)
- Teach sport-specific skills (30) and competitive strategies (32) using varied instructional (31) and motivational techniques (33)
- Assess athlete (34) and program staff (39) performance and adapt planning and instruction accordingly (36)
- Possess good competitive and tactical decision-making skills and incorporate competitive and tactical strategies (26) for performance success
- Model appropriate ethical behavior (7) and demonstrate positive behavior to all officials, coaches, and spectators (29) in accordance with the organization's guidelines
- Demonstrate self-control in competitive situations (37) and a willingness to improve coaching practice through provided training and/or self-education (40–42)
- Identify potential risks associated with the sport (13, 15) and/or participants (14) and adapt practice sessions accordingly (16)
- Promote sound nutritional practices (19), provide accurate information regarding drugs and supplement use, and advocate for a drug-free sport environment (20)
- Understand the appropriate protocol in responding to common injuries (17) and working with trained sport medicine professionals in "Return to Play" procedures following an injury (18)
- Engage in professional development activities (40–42) to improve interpersonal (9), intrapersonal (38), and professional (30) knowledge

Qualifications

- Successful Completion of a Background Check
- CPR/First Aid Certification & Concussion Training (17)
- Safe Sport Training (12)
- A Bachelor's Degree in Coaching or related field
- The highest possible National Coaching Certification or Licensure level from corresponding NGB/HPMO

Preferred Qualifications

- A Master's Degree in Coaching or related field
- 3 to 5 years of experience training high performance athletes

*Corresponding *NSSC* are represented by the numbers in ( ).

Table on Depth and Knowledge of Skills

Table 5.6 depicts what a beginning coach should be able to do, relative to each standard, prior to assuming the role of coach. In addition, **Table 5.6** provides insight into what a coach striving for mastery should be able to do relative to each standard. Table 5.6 is general for all sport contexts. Coach educators/developers and administrators can adapt to the sport and level of competition you work in.

Sample Evaluation Forms

The following evaluation forms offer examples of how an individual providing coach education or coach development can assess the ability and development of their coaches using the *NSSC*.

Sample A: Readiness to Coach Evaluation

The *Readiness to Coach Evaluation* evaluates a coach's prior preparation relative to the 42 standards of the *NSSC* (see **Table 5.7** on page 53). Sport administrators

Table 5.6 Depth of Knowledge/Skills Beginning Coach to Master Coach

NSSC Standards	Developing a Depth of Knowledge and Skills	
	Beginning Coach	Master Coach
Set Vision, Standards, and Goals for the Program	*A beginning coach should be able to...*	*...a coach striving for mastery*
Standard 1 Develop and enact an athlete-centered coaching philosophy	Understand the components of an athlete-centered coaching philosophy and understand how to implement one in practice....	...demonstrates effectiveness over a period of time in developing athletic skills and/or achieving success in competition using an athlete-centered coaching philosophy
Standard 2 Use long-term athlete development with the intent to develop athletic potential, enhance physical literacy, and encourage lifelong physical activity	Identify the appropriate stages of athlete development and employ strategies to help athletes cultivate knowledge and skills for physical literacy and lifelong physical activity...	...effectively applies the principles of long-term athlete development and promotes physical literacy and lifelong enjoyment in the activity through coaching practice and adherence to program standards
Standard 3 Create a unified vision using strategic planning and goal-setting principles	Develop a vision that aligns with personal values and institutional standards in developing the athlete. Establish goals to measure and evaluate progress toward achieving the vision...	...leads others in developing a shared vision for the program and is effective in aligning the vision with goals that focus on learner outcomes related to the physical, behavioral, and social development of the athlete
Standard 4 Align program with all rules and regulations and needs of the community and individual athletes	Adhere to established rules and regulations. Identify the needs of the community and each athlete in the program...	...adapts teaching methods to enforce rules and regulations. Uses interpersonal knowledge to build relationships with community members and individual athletes to best meet their needs
Standard 5 Manage program resources in a responsible manner	Understand which program resources they are responsible for and adhere to organizational policies in fiscal and facility management...	...demonstrates effectiveness in managing resources over an extended period of time.
Engage in and Support Ethical Practices	*A beginning coach should be able to...*	*...a coach striving for mastery*
Standard 6 Abide by the code of conduct within their coaching context	Identify and adhere to ethical standards previously established by the organization and/or professional association...	...role models ethical practice aligned with the code of conduct over an extended period of time

	Beginning Coach — A beginning coach should be able to...	Master Coach — ...a coach striving for mastery
Standard 7 Model, teach, and reinforce ethical behavior with program participants	Identify and model appropriate ethical behavior. Understand strategies for teaching and reinforcing appropriate ethical behavior among program participants...	...role models ethical practice over an extended period of time as well as teaches and reinforces ethical behavior among athletes in practices and competitions
Standard 8 Develop an ethical decision-making process based on ethical standards	Understand the ethical decision-making process and employ strategies to assist them in evaluating and reasoning that is consistent with ethical principles...	...pursues life-long learning activities to enhance understanding of potential ethical dilemmas and demonstrates the ability to reflect upon their action to improve ethical decision-making in the future
Build Relationships	*Beginning Coach* / *A beginning coach should be able to...*	*Master Coach* / *...a coach striving for mastery*
Standard 9 Acquire and utilize interpersonal and communication skills	Demonstrate oral and written communication skills in alignment with organization expectations. Identify specific communication skills they need to improve on...	...effectively applies oral and written communication skills in conjunction with active listening skills to build relationships with all program stakeholders
Standard 10 Develop competencies to work with a diverse group of individuals	Recognize and appreciate physical, mental, and cultural diversity. Understand how one's own background could limit one's ability to work effectively with a diverse group of individuals...	...demonstrates the ability to adapt instructional methods to work with groups and individuals with distinct characteristics and qualities. Effectively uses self-reflection techniques to become more self-aware of potential bias related to their background
Standard 11 Demonstrate professionalism and leadership with all stakeholders	Understand professional standards as established by the organization and/or professional association and implement them during interactions with all stakeholders...	...role models professional standards and engages in self-reflection and self-awareness techniques to continue to develop as a leader
Develop a Safe Sport Environment	*Beginning Coach* / *A beginning coach should be able to...*	*Master Coach* / *...a coach striving for mastery*
Standard 12 Create a respectful and safe environment which is free from harassment and abuse	Identify characteristics of a safe sport environment and understand how to develop a culture free of harassment and abuse...	...educates and engages others in building a welcoming environment. Has established traditions and/or policies to reduce bullying or hazing

(continues)

Table 5.6 Depth of Knowledge/Skills Beginning Coach to Master Coach *(continued)*

NSSC Standards	Developing a Depth of Knowledge and Skills	
Develop a Safe Sport Environment	Beginning Coach	Master Coach
	A beginning coach should be able to...	...a coach striving for mastery
Standard 13 Collaborate with program directors to fulfill all legal responsibilities and risk management procedures associated with coaching	Understand legal responsibilities associated with their position and identify potential risks associated with their sport on and off the field of play...	...demonstrates the ability to apply and adapt professional knowledge in managing potential and unexpected risks of their position
Standard 14 Identify and mitigate physical, psychological, and sociocultural conditions that predispose athletes to injuries	Recognize changes in an athlete's behavior related to physical conditions, health, body structure, poor nutrition, lack of sleep, etc. Adapt training programs or intensity of practice sessions to avoid athlete injury due to changes in an athlete's behavior or demeanor...	...adapts expected athlete outcomes during a practice session in accordance with ever-changing athlete behaviors. Continues to develop professional knowledge on physical, psychological, and sociocultural conditions that impact an athlete's risk
Standard 15 Monitor environmental conditions and modify participation as needed to ensure the health and safety of participants	Understand environmental conditions that could constitute a risk for athletes. Conduct proper protocol in reducing the risk...	...continue to develop professional knowledge on safety guidelines and procedures, while following proper protocol in reducing risk. Demonstrate flexibility in planning, by adapting to unexpected conditions to ensure the proper risk management protocol is being followed
Standard 16 Reduce potential injuries by instituting safe and proper training principles and procedures	Understand safe practice procedures and proper supervision guidelines as set forth by the organization. Recognize physical and physiological factors that may lead to athlete injuries...	...demonstrates knowledge in the training of athletes through safe practice procedures and continues to develop professional knowledge to better recognize the causes of acute and chronic injuries relative to the sport
Standard 17 Develop awareness of common injuries in sport and provide immediate and appropriate care within the scope of practice	Aware of protocols to provide appropriate care. Understand concussion protocol and activate the emergency action plan...	...maintains CPR and first aid certification. Adapts to changes in concussion protocol. Demonstrates professional knowledge when responding to injuries, including referrals to proper health care professionals

	A beginning coach should be able to... (Beginning Coach)	...a coach striving for mastery (Master Coach)
Standard 18 Support the decisions of sports medicine professionals to help athletes have a healthy return to participation following an injury	Understand the appropriate protocol in helping athletes return to play following an injury. Identify strategies to support athletes socially and psychologically in their return to play.	...demonstrates over a period of time the ability to support athletes in returning to play by providing a supportive environment that helps athletes with self-confidence, motivation, and overcoming the fear of re-injury
Standard 19 Model and encourage nutritional practices that ensure the health and safety of athletes	Understand basic, research-based nutritional concepts to promote positive dietary habits. Recognize athletes exhibiting the signs of a potential eating disorders...	...encourages proper nutritional practices among athletes based on sound nutritional advice from experts. Continues to develop professional knowledge on nutritional issues facing athletes (i.e., eating disorders, dietary habits) and stays within scope of practice
Standard 20 Provide accurate information about drugs and supplements to athletes and advocate for drug-free sport participation	Identify current trends in supplement and drug use among athletes. Recognize the signs of an athlete exhibiting potential drug abuse...	...demonstrates professional knowledge in regard to drugs and supplement use among athletes. Intervenes to protect and assist athletes whose performance or health is being impacted by supplement or drug use
Create a Positive and Inclusive Sport Environment	*Beginning Coach* *A beginning coach should be able to...*	*Master Coach* *...a coach striving for mastery*
Standard 21 Implement a positive and enjoyable sport climate based on best practices for psychosocial and motivational principles to maximize athlete and team well-being and performance	Develop a positive sport climate by emphasizing effort, learning, and promoting life-long physical activity. Encourage personal responsibility to help athletes develop decision-making skills and build confidence...	...demonstrates the ability to create a positive and enjoyable sport climate that emphasizes personal and performance excellence, promotes life-long physical activity, and well-being
Standard 22 Build inclusive practices into the program for all which are aligned with current legal and ethical guidelines	Adhere to legal guidelines related to athlete eligibility and participation opportunities. Understand ethical implications related to inclusive practices...	...role models and aligns practice to encourage the participation of varying groups and adhere to current legal and ethical guidelines
Standard 23 Understand the importance of including athletes with disabilities in meaningful participation in established sport programs and consider options for athletes who cannot participate in traditional sport opportunities	Appreciate the importance of including athletes with disabilities and devise accommodations within the sport organization's guidelines to provide participation opportunities...	...demonstrates over time the willingness to adapt the sport program to provide accommodations for athletes who cannot participate in traditional sport opportunities. Continues to develop professional knowledge to better recognize scenarios and opportunities for athletes with disabilities within sport program

(continues)

(continued)

Table 5.6 Depth of Knowledge/Skills Beginning Coach to Master Coach

NSSC Standards	Developing a Depth of Knowledge and Skills	
	Beginning Coach	Master Coach →
Conduct Practices and Prepare for Competition --- PLAN ---	A beginning coach should be able to...	...a coach striving for mastery
Standard 24 Create seasonal and/or annual plans that incorporate developmentally appropriate progressions for instructing sport-specific skills based on best practices in motor development, biomechanics, and motor learning	Develop a skill progression plan for the season and/or a calendar year which includes appropriate sport-specific technical and tactical skills for the season...	...demonstrates expert knowledge in planning a sport-specific skill progression plan for the season and/or calendar year. Continues to develop professional knowledge in the areas of motor development, biomechanics, and motor learning to stay current on best practices
Standard 25 Design appropriate progressions for improving sport-specific physiological systems throughout all phases of the sport season using essential principles of exercise physiology and nutritional knowledge	Design a training and/or conditioning progression plan for the sport season that utilizes physiological and biomechanical principles, in addition to nutritional guidelines...	...demonstrates expert knowledge in planning a training and/or conditioning progression plan for the sport season. Continues to develop professional knowledge in the areas of physiological and biomechanical principles, in addition to nutritional guidelines to stay current on best practices
Standard 26 Plan practices to incorporate appropriate competition strategies, tactics, and scouting information	Design a practice session with an appropriate mix of technical and tactical instruction relative to the sport and competitive level.	...demonstrates expert knowledge in designing practice sessions that develop competence in athletes through an effective mix of technical and tactical instruction
Standard 27 Incorporate mental skills into practice and competition to enhance performance and athlete well-being	Aware of the types of mental skill training that could be implemented into practice and competition settings...	...effectively implements mental skill training techniques into practice and competition settings, while aligning with learner outcomes that build confidence and competence
Standard 28 Create intentional strategies to develop life skills and promote their transfer to other life domains	Recognize opportunities to teach life skills in practice and competitive settings. Identify strategies for teaching life skills...	...deliberately instills life skill training into practice and competition settings
Standard 29 Understand components of effective contest management	Understands their role in preparing facilities, securing officials, and promoting positive behavior relative to the organization they work for...	...role models appropriate behavior to all stakeholders and mentors less experienced coaches in effectively preparing for competition

	A beginning coach should be able to...	...a coach striving for mastery
--- TEACH ---		
Standard 30 Know the skills, elements of skill combinations and techniques, competition strategies and tactics, and the rules associated with the sport being coached	Understand the sport specific skills, competitive strategies, and the rules associated with their sport...	...demonstrates effectiveness and expertise in sport specific skills, competitive strategies, and the rules associated with their sport. Continues to develop professional knowledge relative to these skills and rules to effectively assist athletes in developing competence and confidence
Standard 31 Develop and utilize pedagogical strategies in daily practices	Implement varied instructional techniques to teach sport specific skills and competitive strategies...	...demonstrates effectiveness and expertise in implementing varied instructional techniques to teach sport specific skills and competitive strategies. Continues to develop professional knowledge relative to these techniques to effectively assist athletes in developing competence and confidence
Standard 32 Craft daily practice plans based on sound teaching and learning principles to promote athlete development and optimize competitive performance	Create a daily practice plan following best practice plan guidelines...	...creates a daily practice plan following best practice guidelines and assesses the plan through reflection to ensure the practice session meets learner outcomes
Standard 33 Use appropriate motivational techniques to enhance performance and athlete engagement during practices and competitions	Understand and apply appropriate motivational techniques related to individual differences and practice and competitive settings....	...demonstrates effectiveness in employing motivational techniques specific to the individual athlete within practice and competitive setting
--- Assess ---		
Standard 34 Implement appropriate strategies for evaluating athlete training, development, and performance	Understand strategies and tools for assessing athletes. Devise or implement tools relative to the sport and/or organization...	...implements assessment instruments to capture data on athlete performance and training to adjust instructional practices to best meet athlete outcomes
Standard 35 Engage athletes in a process of continuous self-assessment and reflection to foster responsibility for their own learning and development	Identify tools athletes can use to self-assess and implement them in practice...	...encourages athlete self-assessment through effective instructional practices to bolster athlete confidence, cultivate critical decision making and personal accountability, and foster the importance of lifelong learning

(continues)

(continued)

Table 5.6 Depth of Knowledge/Skills Beginning Coach to Master Coach

NSSC Standards	Developing a Depth of Knowledge and Skills	...a coach striving for mastery
--- Adapt ---	A beginning coach should be able to...	
Standard 36 Adjust training and competition plans based on athlete needs and assessment practices	Based on evaluation of athlete skill progression, physical and mental health, and goals, adjusts teaching and training methods accordingly...	...demonstrates effectiveness and expertise over time in the ability to adapt practice sessions to meet the needs of the learner
Standard 37 Use strategic decision-making skills to make adjustments, improvements, or change course throughout a competition	Identify strategic decision-making moments in competition and demonstrate self-control in making strategic decisions...	...demonstrates effectiveness and expertise over time in the ability to make decisions during competition and maintain self-control
Strive for Continuous Improvement*	*Beginning Coach* — Master Coach →	*Master Coach*
	A beginning coach should be able to...	...a coach striving for mastery
Standard 38 Regularly engage in self-reflection or peer-reflection to deeply examine situations, generate potential solutions, and think through those solutions	Identify self-reflection techniques and be able to apply them to improve coach practice....	...engages regularly in self-reflection techniques to assist in making strategic decisions. Communicates with other coaches and/or mentors for support in making tough decisions
Standard 39 Develop an evaluation strategy to monitor and improve staff and team performance	Identify a variety of methods for evaluating their program including student-athlete performance, coach effectiveness, etc. Develop a method to implement ongoing evaluation...	...implements a variety of evaluation instruments in regard to the program and reflections to self-monitor their ability to improve team and staff performance
Standard 40 Improve coaching effectiveness by seeking to learn the latest information on coaching through various avenues of coach development	Identify resources and engage in professional development opportunities...	...demonstrates a willingness to pursue learning opportunities in search of increased professional, intrapersonal, and interpersonal knowledge
Standard 41 Engage in mentoring and communities of practice to promote a learning culture and continual improvement	Identify and engage with potential mentors and groups of coaches in which they can seek continual guidance and support....	...leads groups of coaches through informal discussion to improve coaching practice and has established mentors they can reach out to for advice or assistance
Standard 42 Maintain work-life harmony and practice self-care to manage stress and burnout	Identify and develop strategies for preserving work-life harmony...	...demonstrate and adapt physical and mental strategies to role-model work-life harmony

*National Standards for Sport Coaches, SHAPE America. Retrieved from https://www.shapeamerica.org/uploads/pdfs/2018/standards/National-Standards-for-Sport-Coaches-DRAFT.pdf

or anyone in the position of hiring coaches can use this form to evaluate candidates for coaching positions and/or in evaluating how much training a new hire needs to be prepared to coach relative to the *NSSC*. The evaluation is applicable to any context and can be modified as needed.

Sample B: Season Practice Observational Tool

The *Season Practice Observational Tool* is an example of a method for assessing the ability of the coach to provide instruction relative to the *NSSC* and the sport being coached (see **Table 5.8** on page 55). This assessment could be used by coach educators, coach developers, and/or sport administrators.

Sample C: Professional Development Checklist

The *Professional Development Checklist* can be used to help the coach strive for continuous improvement relative to the *NSSC* (see **Table 5.9** on page 56). The

checklist can be modified for varied sport settings and can be used by coaches, coach educators, coach developers, and/or sport administrators.

Sample D: Safe and Inclusive Environment Self-Assessment

The *Safe and Inclusive Environment Self-Assessment* is a self-reflective exercise for coaches to evaluate their ability to create a safe, risk-free, drug-free, and inclusive learning environment (See **Table 5.10** on page 58). This self-assessment is applicable to all settings.

Sample E: Sport Program Management Evaluation

The *Sport Program Management Evaluation* is an example of an evaluation method for the sport administrator or coach developer to assess the ability of the coach to manage program resources and align with the mission and vision of the sport organization and/or governing body (See **Table 5.11** on page 59). The evaluation form can be modified for a variety of sport contexts.

Table 5.7 Sample A: Evaluation on Readiness to Coach

Instructions: Evaluate a newly hired coach on each category related to the *NSSC*. The *NSSC* are abbreviated here and the ( ) represent the corresponding standard. To score place a "1" if they meet the category relative to the standard and a "0" if they do not meet the category or you cannot determine. Each standard is evaluated based on the following category descriptions:

- **Educational Background:** The coach has a specific training relative to this standard (i.e., degree, certification, certificate, licensure).
- **Coaching Experience:** The coach has coaching experience relative to this standard.
- **Ready:** The coach requires no additional training in this area or this category is not applicable to the role of the coach.

The coach is ready to...	Educational Background	Coaching Experience	Ready	Score
Example of how to score	0	1	0	1
Use an athlete-centered coach philosophy (1)				
Use long-term athlete development principles (2)				
Create a unified vision (3)				
Align program with rules and regulations (4)				
Manage program resources (5)				
Abide by code of conduct (6)				
Model, teach, and reinforce ethical behavior (7)				
Develop an ethical decision-making process (8)				
Acquire and utilize interpersonal communication (9)				
Develop competencies to work with a diverse (10)				

(continues)

Table 5.7 Sample A: Evaluation on Readiness to Coach   (continued)

The coach is ready to...	Educational Background	Coaching Experience	Ready	Score
Example of how to score	0	1	0	1
Demonstrates professionalism (11)				
Create a respectful and safe environment (12)				
Collaborate with program directors to fulfill legal responsibilities (13)				
Identify and mitigate physical, psychological, and sociocultural conditions (14)				
Monitor environmental conditions (15)				
Reduce potential injuries (16)				
Identify common injuries (17)				
Understand how to support sport medicine professionals' decisions when athlete's return from injury (18)				
Model and encourage sound nutritional practices (19)				
Provide accurate information about drugs and supplements (20)				
Implement a positive and enjoyable sport climate (21)				
Build inclusive practices into the program (22)				
Understand the importance of including athletes with disabilities (23)				
Create seasonal and annual plans (24)				
Design appropriate progressions for improving sport-specific physiological systems (25)				
Plan practices to incorporate appropriate competition strategies (26)				
Incorporate mental skills training (27)				
Create intentional strategies to develop life skills (28)				
Understand components of effective contest management (29)				
Know the skills associated with the sport being coached (30)				
Develop and utilize pedagogical strategies (31)				
Craft daily practice plans (32)				
Use appropriate motivational techniques (33)				
Implement appropriate strategies for evaluating athlete training, development, and performance (34)				
Engage athletes in a process of continuous self-assessment (35)				
Adjust training and competition plans based on athlete needs (36)				
Use strategic decision-making skills (37)				
Regularly engage in self-reflection (38)				
Develop an evaluation strategy to monitor (39)				

The coach is ready to...	Educational Background	Coaching Experience	Ready	Score
Example of how to score	0	1	0	1
Improve coaching effectiveness (40)				
Engage in mentoring (41)				
Maintain work–life harmony (42)				
Total Score				

0–21: Not ready for coaching role
22–62: Needs additional training before being considered for coaching role
63–104: Hire and provide training prior to working with athletes
105–126: Ready for coaching role, provide ongoing training for professional development

Table 5.8 **Sample B: Season Practice Observational Tool**

Instructions: These checklists contain skills associated with some of the *NSSC* and the () represents the corresponding standard within the *NSSC*. The sport administrator can observe a coach in practice and check if they observe the following actions during practice. If an action is not applicable check NA.

✓	During the instructional session, the coach demonstrated the ability to...	NA
	Teach the appropriate techniques for physical skill development (30)	
	Teach competitive strategies relative to the age and development level of the athletes (30)	
	Accurately teach and reinforce the rules of the sport (30)	
	Utilize a variety of instructional methods to teach technical skills (31)	
	Utilize a variety of instructional methods to teach tactical skills (31)	
	Provide feedback that emphasizes effort (33)	
	Provide feedback that is positive and corrective (33)	
	Encourage and foster athlete decision-making (35)	
	Develop or teach a mental skill (self-talk, goal-setting, imagery) (27)	
	Teach a life skill (e.g., effort, teamwork, leadership) (28)	
	Make adjustments during practice based on the needs of the athletes (i.e., fatigue, emotional state, etc.) (36)	
	Design an effective practice session that includes by (30, 32)	
	Opening comments that clearly outline expectations/objectives	
	Warm-up	
	Drills and activities are designed to keep athletes active	
	Simulations of the competition setting	
	Appropriate progression of drills and games throughout practice	
	Adjustments to provide appropriate challenge for all athletes	
	Effective behavioral management techniques	
	Checking for athlete understanding	
	Cool down	
	Closing comments	

Post-Observation Questions

Sport administrators can use these questions to guide the discussion that follows an observation.

1. What were your main objectives in the practice session?
2. Describe some things you believe went well during the practice (once the coach responds, the administrator might add additional positive observations).
3. What elements of your coaching in that practice do you think could have gone better? (administrator may add additional areas for improvement …but only if necessary)
4. What are the areas of coaching that you are still working on that I can support?

Table 5.9 Sample C: Professional Development Evaluation

Instructions: This form can be used by the coach, sport administrator, coach educator, or coach developer to assess the progress of a coach in regard to their professional development and offer action steps for improvement.

✓	The coach knows how to...	Action Steps for Improvement
	Develop and enact an athlete-centered coaching philosophy (1)	
	Use long-term athlete development concepts (2)	
	Create a unified vision for the program for the physical, behavioral, and social development of the athlete (3)	
	Align the program with all rules and regulations associated with the sport (4)	
	Manage program resources (5)	
	Abide by the code of conduct within their coaching context (6)	
	Model and reinforce appropriate ethical behavior (7)	
	Evaluate decision-making options using ethical approaches (8)	
	Use oral and written communication skills to communicate effectively with all stakeholders (9)	
	Build positive relationships with all stakeholders (9)	
	Create a respectful and safe environment free from harassment and abuse (12)	
	Fulfill all legal responsibilities and risk management procedures (13)	
	Identify and mitigate physical, psychological, and sociocultural conditions that predispose athletes to injuries (14)	
	Monitor environmental conditions and modify participation as needed to ensure the health and safety of participants (15)	
	Reduce potential injuries by instituting safe and proper training principles and procedures (16)	
	Provide immediate and appropriate care, within the scope of practice, when responding to common injuries in sport (17)	
	Model and encourage appropriate nutritional practices (19)	
	Provide accurate information about drugs and supplements to athletes and advocate for drug-free sport participation (20)	
	Implement a positive and enjoyable sport climate (21)	

✓	The coach knows how to...	Action Steps for Improvement
	Build inclusive practices into the program for all groups (22)	
	Understand the importance of including athletes with disabilities in meaningful participation (23)	
	Create seasonal and/or annual plans that incorporate developmentally appropriate progressions for instructing sport-specific skills based on best practices (24)	
	Design appropriate progressions for improving sport-specific physiological systems throughout all phases of the sport season (25)	
	Plan practices to incorporate appropriate competition strategies, tactics, and scouting information (26)	
	Incorporate mental skills into practice and competition to enhance performance and athlete well-being (27)	
	Develop life skills and promote their transfer to other life domains (28)	
	Understand components of effective contest management (29)	
	Develop and utilize pedagogical strategies in daily practices (31)	
	Craft daily practice plans based on sound teaching and learning principles to promote athlete development and optimize competitive performance (32)	
	Use appropriate motivational techniques to enhance performance during practices and competitions (33)	
	Implement appropriate strategies for evaluating athlete training, development, and performance (34)	
	Adjust training and competition plans based on athlete needs and assessment practices (36)	
	Use strategic decision-making skills to make adjustments, improvements, or change course throughout a competition (37)	
	Regularly engage in self-reflection or peer-reflection to deeply examine situations, generate potential solutions, and think through those solutions (38)	
	Develop an evaluation strategy to monitor and improve staff and team performance (39)	
	Implement a performance improvement plan to evaluate what they need to learn (40)	
	Engage athletes in a process of continuous self-assessment and reflection to foster responsibility for their own learning (41)	
	Maintain work–life harmony and practice self-care to manage stress and burnout (42)	
	Practice self-reflection exercises to identify stress in their life (42)	
	Practice self-reflection exercises to identify potential signs of burnout (42)	

Table 5.10 Sample D: Safe and Inclusive Environment

Instructions: This is a self-reflective exercise for coaches to evaluate their ability to create a safe, risk-free, drug-free, and inclusive learning environment. This self-assessment is applicable to all settings.

As a coach I...	Yes	Need to Improve	Not Sure How to Do This*
treat athletes and staff with respect (12)			
reduce potential for physical or mental abuse towards athletes from others (12)			
reduce potential for sexual harassment toward athletes from others (12)			
prevent and monitor potential bullying and/or hazing (12)			
identify and minimize potential risks associated with my sport (13)			
am aware of how an athlete's health status, body structure and periods of growth can predispose them to injury (14)			
am aware of how physical conditions can predispose an athlete to injury (14)			
am aware of how an athlete's current condition (i.e., lack of sleep, fatigue, poor nutrition, and/or emotional state) could warrant a change in the practice plan (14)			
follow established standards and protocol in monitoring environmental conditions (i.e., heat, cold, lightening) as when to modify or stop play (15)			
ensure safe facilities and equipment (16)			
institute safe practice procedures and supervise athletes during practice (16)			
recognize biomechanical factors that underlie the causes of injuries (16)			
follow proper physiological training principles to avoid overtraining (16)			
am trained in CPR/First Aid (17)			
am trained in concussion awareness (17)			
can activate the emergency action plan when responding to an injury and/or refer an athlete to proper healthcare professionals (17)			
support decisions of sport medicine professionals when athletes return to play from an injury (18)			
provide a supportive environment (i.e., socially, psychologically) during athlete rehabilitation as they return to play (18)			
model a healthy lifestyle (19)			
promote dietary habits that fuel the athlete in a safe and healthy manner (19)			
promote dietary habits that encourage a healthy body image (19)			
am proactive in identifying potential eating disorders and referring when necessary (19)			
provide accurate information about drugs and supplements (20)			
intervene and/or refer athletes to appropriate experts when changes in body composition, physical appearance, and or uncharacteristic behaviors that may be drug-related are observed (20)			
create a positive climate by emphasizing effort and learning (21)			

As a coach I...	Yes	Need to Improve	Not Sure How to Do This*
keep winning in perspective (21)			
challenge athletes to improve their skills in a supportive environment (21)			
encourage personal responsibility and athlete decision-making (21)			
provide assistance and referral for mental health issues (21)			
welcome all eligible athletes and use strategies to encourage participation (22)			
value the contribution of all athletes including those from underrepresented and disadvantaged groups (22)			
follow legal and ethical guidelines to ensure all athletes have equal opportunity to participate (22)			
build inclusive practices into the program (22)			
include athletes with disabilities with necessary accommodations that do not interfere with the integrity of the game or equal opportunities for all athletes, with and without disabilities, to be competitive (23)			
work with administrators to provide appropriate alternatives if athletes with disabilities cannot participate in the traditional version of the sport (23)			

*During reflection, if you are unsure on how to meet this standard refer to Section 3.

Table 5.11 Sample E: Program Management Evaluation

Instructions: Evaluate the coach on each of the following items related to program management, by placing an "X" in the appropriate box. Rather than trying to see what the coach cannot do, administrators should make every attempt to gain evidence of a coach's ability to demonstrate each of the behaviors below. This may require additional forms of evidence (e.g., sample handouts, practice observations, parent and athlete comments, etc.). However, if a coach does not demonstrate these behaviors, consider educational opportunities to help the coach improve in these areas.

The coach demonstrates the ability to...	Needs Improvement	Average	Excellent
Establish Program Standards and Model Behavior			
Align the program to match the needs of the athlete and the community (4)			
Follow all applicable rules (i.e., national, regional, institutional) and regulations to ensure program is in compliance (4)			
Adhere to all rules and regulations in regard to athlete eligibility (4)			
Manage the program budget in alignment with organizational policies (5)			
Manage the program facilities in alignment with organizational policies (5)			
Abide by the code of conduct established by the governing body of their sport (5)			
Abide by the code of conduct established by the organization (5)			
Model appropriate ethical behavior (7)			
Reinforce ethical behavior with program participants (7)			

(continues)

Table 5.11 **Sample E: Program Management Evaluation** *(continued)*

The coach demonstrates the ability to...	Needs Improvement	Average	Excellent
Build Relationships			
Develop positive coach–athlete relationships (9)			
Elicit community support for the program (9)			
Maintain self-control in working with others (9)			
Demonstrate professionalism in working with all stakeholders (11)			
Create a Positive, Inclusive, and Safe Environment			
Create a respectful and safe environment free from harassment and abuse (12)			
Prevent and monitor potential bullying and/or hazing (12)			
Identify and minimize potential risks associated with the sport (13)			
Supervise athletes during practice (16)			
Implement safe and proper training principles and procedures (16)			
Support decisions of sport medicine professionals in helping athletes return to play (18)			
Create a positive and enjoyable climate based on best practices related to the age and development of the participants (21)			
Follow legal (e.g., ADA, Title IX) guidelines to ensure all athletes have equal opportunity to participate (22)			
Communicate with administrators to accommodate athletes with disabilities (23)			
Manage Practice and Competitions			
Prepare facilities for competition (29)			
Model positive behavior to all officials, opposing coaches, and spectators during competition (29)			
Create and document daily practice plans (32)			
Provide transparency in athlete selection and squad size (34)			
Evaluate and provide support for program staff (39)			
Supervise and monitor the performance of program staff (39)			

© Luradio/E-/Getty Images.

SECTION 6

Glossary

Athlete-centered coaching A philosophical approach to coaching that focuses on the development of the whole athlete (i.e., physical, psychological, and social-emotional development), where sport coaches prioritize opportunities for development over winning because they recognize that this helps athletes reach their full potential as human beings and creates sustainable success for the program.

Best practices Activities or styles that have been deemed appropriate by the profession and result in positive outcomes. (from 2nd edition)

Coach A sport coach is an individual tasked with creating a quality sport experience which guides the physical, psychological, and social-emotional development of athletes on their team (Lyle & Cushion, 2017) relative to the level and type of sport they coach.

Coaching associations A membership-based organization that provides benefits to member coaches through coaching resources, professional development training, networking, and job placement.

Coach developer An umbrella term for those who are trained to support coaches in their ongoing professional development at all phases of their career (International Council for Coaching Excellence (ICCE), the Association of Summer Olympic Federations (ASOIF) & Leeds Metropolitan University, 2014). A coach developer has expertise in their field and understands the learning process and adult learners. Their roles include designing and evaluating educational programs, facilitating learning experiences for coaches, assessing coaches to encourage further professional development, and mentoring coaches.

Coach educator Individuals trained for and tasked with delivering or facilitating formal coach education (e.g., clinics, courses, and workshops) and evaluating the effectiveness of these educational endeavors.

Examples of coaching educators include collegiate faculty, directors of coaching education, workshop facilitators, etc.

Coach education Formal and non-formal learning experiences that support the development of knowledge, skills, behaviors, and values associated with effective coach practice. These experiences should take into account coaches' experiences and coaching context and align with best practices in coaching (e.g., NSSC).

Coach effectiveness "The consistent application of integrated professional, interpersonal, and intrapersonal knowledge to improve athletes' competence, confidence, connection, and character in specific coaching contexts" (Côté & Gilbert, 2009, p. 316).

College/University athletic departments Public or private higher education institutions that provide support for intercollegiate athletic competition and provide professional development opportunities for coaches.

Communities of practice A situated learning experience in which a group of individuals, engaged in a similar profession, develop their knowledge and expertise through their shared interactions over time.

Continuous improvement A recognition that coaches are continually engaging in methods to improve their practice over time whether that be from self-directed learning, reflection, or formal and non-formal learning experiences.

Core responsibilities The essential job duties for which coaches are accountable in coaching practice.

Evaluation A systematic process by which a person judges the quality of current practice based on a set of criteria. A formative evaluation involves use of observable and measurable criteria to determine areas of improvement.

Exercise physiology The study of the processes and functions of the human body as influenced by the performance of any physical activity. (from 2nd edition)

Fiscal management Planning and using resources in accordance with established policies and regulations.

Games-based learning Using the context of a game to introduce or refine skills, tactics, or decision-making. This requires modification or regulation of game play to accomplish specific tactical objectives.

Hazing Any action or event conducted with the purpose of ridiculing or humiliating individuals for the intent of group initiation, and which may be harmful and/or illegal. (from 2nd edition)

High school athletic departments Public or private schools that offer sport participation opportunities for adolescents (ages 13–18) and provide support for coaches.

Higher education institutions Long-term coach education programs that are based in an academic setting. These programs range from a minor in an undergraduate program, full undergraduate majors, or master's degrees in sport coaching. The programs are typically multi-sport.

Life skills Behavioral, cognitive, and social skills that can be developed through sport and transferred to other areas of life.

Long-term athlete development Best practice guidelines for training athletes based on age and stage of development. Promotes physical literacy and life-long physical activity.

Mental skills Learned systematic regulation of cognitive processes to enhance performance, increase enjoyment, and/or achieve self-satisfaction. (from 2nd edition)

Mentoring A formal or informal process by which a mentor, typically a more experienced coach, helps another person (i.e., the mentee) develop in aspects of their coaching practice through modeling, dialogue, observation, guidance, and support.

Multi-sport independent organization Organizations that provide training to coaches across a wide range of sports and age levels.

National Governing Body (NGB) Sport organizations that govern a particular sport (e.g., rules, policies, sanctions, etc.) in a particular country under the auspices of the United States Olympic and Paralympic Committee. The NGBs are often the source of education requirements for coaches in their sport participation pathway.

Organization An institution and/or governing body representing the appropriate context. For example, a K-12 school district, collegiate athletic department, non-profit sport clubs, recreation programs, etc.

Pedagogy General concepts, theories, and research about effective teaching. (from 2nd edition)

Performance indicators Evidence of behaviors that reflect understanding of knowledge and mastery of skills in a specific area. (from 2nd edition)

Periodization Division of the yearly training plan into smaller, easier to manage training phases with load that increase progressively and cyclically to optimize performance. Training is designed to allow for overload and adaptation by the inclusion of recovery techniques throughout the program. (from 2nd edition)

Physical literacy A physically literate person has "the motivation, confidence, physical competence, knowledge and understanding to value and take responsibility for maintaining purposeful physical pursuits/activities throughout the lifecourse" (Whitehead, 2013, p. 29).

Psychosocial Combination of the influence of psychological and social factors on individual behavior.

Reflective practice Practices incorporated by coaches to solve coaching problems. It entails identifying the coaching issues, reflecting on possible solutions in isolation or collaboration with others, testing out solutions and evaluating their effectiveness.

Self-care Practices incorporated by coaches to maintain their own well-being and work–life harmony.

Scouting Methods of evaluating upcoming opponents to better prepare athletes for competition. Some techniques that can be used include observation, video, and statistical review. In terms of youth sport, this could be as simple as evaluating whether or not the opposing team has enough players to field a team for a game. (from 2nd edition)

Sport administrator An individual that oversees the management of sport program operations and supervises coaches through hiring, training, and evaluation. Examples of sport administrators include: Activity Directors, Athletics Directors, Associate/Assistant Athletic Directors, Directors of Youth Sport Programs (non-profit or for profit), and High Performance Directors.

Stakeholders Individuals with an interest in or direct involvement in a sport program, including the athletes, coach, parents, administrators, officials, support staff, coaching staff, etc.

Standards (Competencies) The observable and measurable knowledge (i.e., professional knowledge, interpersonal knowledge, and intrapersonal knowledge), skills, and values that guide best practices in sport coaching.

Strategic decision-making Competitive decisions made by an individual or team about overall play of the game. (from 2nd edition)

Tactics An individual or team's actions about when, why, and how to respond to a particular game situation.

Youth sport organizations (Ages 6–14) Public or private organizations that offer organized multisport or single sport experiences for youth and provide educational opportunities for coaches.

REFERENCES

Whitehead, M. (2013). Definition of physical literacy and clarification of related. *ICSSPE Bulletin, Journal of Sport Science & Physical Education, 65*, 28–33.

Côté, J., & Gilbert, W. (2009). An integrative definition of coaching effectiveness and expertise. *International Journal of Sports Science & Coaching, 4*, 307–323.

International Council for Coaching Excellence (ICCE), the Association of Summer Olympic Federations (ASOIF) and

Leeds Metropolitan University (2013). *International sport coaching framework.* Human Kinetics.

Lyle, J., & Cushion, C. (2017). *Sport coaching concepts: A framework for coaching practice* (2nd ed.). Routledge.

National Association for Sport and Physical Education (NASPE) (2006). *Quality coaches, quality sports: National standards for sport coaches.* (2nd ed.). Author.

© Lisa Kolbasa/Shutterstock

Appendix A

Accredited Coach Education Programs

All of the programs listed here have been accredited through the National Committee for the Accreditation of Coaching Education (NCACE). The accreditation process provides an external evaluation of the coach education program to determine whether a program meets or exceeds established criteria for accreditation as documented in the NCACE Guidelines for Accreditation and the standards established in the National Standards for Sport Coaches (2006).

- ACEing Autism
- American Youth Soccer Organization
- Bridgewater College
- Clarion University
- Emporia State University
- Georgia Southern University
- Institute for Rowing Leadership
- James Madison University
- Kutztown University
- Professional Tennis Registry
- Smith College
- Southern Arkansas University
- Special Olympics North America
- University of Central Florida
- University of Northern Colorado
- University of Southern Mississippi
- USA Football
- USA Track & Field
- United States Sports Academy
- Western Michigan University

Registry of Accredited Programs, National Committee for Accreditation of Coaching Education (NCACE), Retrieved from https://www.quality coachingeducation.org/accredited-programs/

The following are approved providers for domain-specific accreditation:

- Cheer Conditioning Academy—(Domain 3: Physical Conditioning and Domain 5: Teaching and Communication)
- Classical Academy of Arms—(Domain 6: Sport Skills & Tactics)
- U.S. Anti-Doping Agency's TrueSport Program —(Domain 1: Philosophy and Ethics)
- Play Like A Champion—(Domain 1: Philosophy and Ethics, and Domain 4: Growth & Development for Sport as Ministry Program; Domain 1: Philosophy & Ethics for Play Like a Champion Today High School Program))
- U.S. Track & Field and Cross-Country Coaches Association—(Domain 3: Physical Conditioning)

Appendix B

Connections Between Standards Across Editions

Standards (Third Edition)	Standards (Second Edition)	Standards (Third Edition)	Standards (Second Edition)
Standard 1	Standard 1	Standard 22	Standards 19, 36
Standard 2	Standard 16	Standard 23	Standard 36
Standard 3	Standard 20	Standard 24	Standards 12, 16, 21
Standard 4		Standard 25	Standards 12, 13, 21
Standard 5	Standards 32, 33, 35	Standard 26	Standard 28
Standard 6	Standard 3	Standard 27	Standard 24
Standard 7	Standards 2, 3, 4	Standard 28	Standards 2, 3, 17, 18
Standard 8	Standard 3	Standard 29	Standard 30
Standard 9	Standards 25, 31	Standard 30	Standard 27
Standard 10	Standard 19	Standard 31	Standards 23, 27
Standard 11	Standards 4, 25	Standard 32	Standards 22, 25
Standard 12	Standards 2, 3, 4, 19	Standard 33	Standards 17, 19, 23, 26
Standard 13	Standard 36	Standard 34	Standards 23, 38, 39
Standard 14	Standards 8, 13	Standard 35	Standards 18, 38, 39
Standard 15	Standard 7	Standard 36	Standards 12, 13, 16, 27
Standard 16	Standards 5, 6, 17	Standard 37	Standards 28, 29
Standard 17	Standards 9, 10, 34	Standard 38	Standard 40
Standard 18	Standards 11, 15	Standard 39	Standards 37, 40
Standard 19	Standard 13	Standard 40	
Standard 20	Standard 14	Standard 41	
Standard 21	Standards 17, 19, 20, 26	Standard 42	

Index